Extraordinary Times
Extraordinary Beings

Extraordinary Times
Extraordinary Beings

Experiences of an American
diplomat with Maitreya and the
Masters of Wisdom

Wayne S. Peterson

Emergence Press

Published by Emergence Press, Henderson, Nevada USA
Published 2001
ISBN 0-9705610-0-8

Printed in the United States of America

The cover painting is by the author who was influenced by the spiritual artist Nicholas Roerich (1874-1947). The Himalayan mountains were a major inspiration for many of Roerich's paintings. The area is rich in legend and often referred to in esoteric spiritual writings. In this painting, Mr. Peterson has taken advantage of the Tibetan legend of the 'steed of happiness'.

The white horse descends from the mountains, along with Maitreya, into the world of mankind below. The horse carries on its back the sacred stone Chintamani—the treasure of the world—and the sacred flame or Agni. Together, Maitreya, along with his Masters of Wisdom, bring the flame of enlightenment to all humanity. In this new era the Divine Fire has now been brought out of the mountains to illumine human consciousness.

ᕫ Contents ᕬ

CONTENTS

both dramatic change and undreamed of potential. The
next step is up to us.

As old as mankind, these ancient ideas predict and
describe the events now unfolding. I review them and
their modern teachers.

❧ Illustrations ❧

Note: Some of the photos reproduced in this book have been widely circulated around the world, and the names or locations of the photographers are not generally known. I include them here with no intent to infringe anyone's copyright but in the spirit of sharing with a larger audience the hope and blessing these images represent to many. I have absolutely no doubt that the extraordinary occurrences depicted are genuine spiritual phenomena and not tricks of photography.

ꙮ Preface ꙮ

From the ending of the cold war to negotiations for a Palestinian homeland, dramatic and unexpected changes have characterized the last decade of this century. For over 32 years, first as a member of the Peace Corps and the U.S. Diplomatic Service, and later as a director of the Fulbright Scholarship Program, I have had a special vantage point and perspective on this tide of changes that has swept over the world. I have seen first-hand some of the most devastating problems and been a party to a few relatively simple solutions which ended up improving the lives of millions of people. Experience has taught me what remains to be done to create a world that works for *everyone*.

During these extraordinary times, while engaged in government service, I was drawn into a personal journey from what one might call the worldly 'halls of power' to a realm of infinitely greater power and splendour, esoterically known as the Hall of Wisdom. In this latter 'supra-world' one is concerned with the *inner* side of life, the indwelling spiritual essence which, through continuous expansion of consciousness, can intuitively distinguish between the true and the false, the real and the unreal, and give one a quality of life undreamed of by most people today.

What I did not initially know was that many of my colleagues in government and diplomatic circles had had similar experiences and had also been contacted by members of a group of extraordinary beings, who might be called the elder brothers of humanity, custodians of the Divine Plan for our evolution. World leaders who are household names have privately confirmed their knowledge of and cooperation with this unfolding plan. And many thousands of ordinary people from all walks of life have seen, experienced, or spoken directly with one or more of these Perfected Men.

It is my intention not only to share with you my *personal* experiences with these beneficent Teachers, but also to provide you with a glimpse into their vast mission and the opportunities we have for collaboration.

The Path upon which I have trodden, at first unknowingly and later with serious intent, is open to *all* seekers after Truth and has nothing to do with one's religious affiliation or life circumstances. It is a journey of self-discovery that never ends.

Combining my experience in both the 'outer' and 'inner' worlds, and in spite of what the evening news might suggest, I have come to a place of deep conviction that the future is bright indeed. As my story unfolds in the following pages you will discover the basis for my optimism and may, perhaps, be inspired to look more deeply into the considerable body of knowledge about this 'Ageless Wisdom' which is as near as your local bookstore, your computer—or your true Self.

I wish to express special thanks to Mr. Benjamin Creme of London for introducing me to the Ageless Wisdom Teachings and providing me, and countless others around the world, with ongoing details about the emergence of these great Teachers. I am also grateful for the valuable assistance and encouragement I received from the many people who believe my experiences are meaningful and uplifting to both those who wonder and those who worry what the future holds in store.

Chapter 1

✤ A Message from Mary ✤

"Wonder is the feeling of a philosopher,
and philosophy begins in wonder."
—Socrates

It all began at Christmas when I had not yet reached my fourth birthday. As a child of three, the preparations for Christmas all appeared so extravagant but very welcome in an otherwise bleak, cold Wisconsin winter.

On Christmas Eve I remember asking my mother what purpose this all served. I recall not understanding why so much effort was being made to celebrate the birthday of someone called Jesus, the Christ child. However, while my mother arranged the small plaster statues of the holy family and accompanying figures of shepherds, animals and three wise men under the Christmas tree, she explained as best she could to a three-year-old that celebrating the Christ child's birth was a reminder of how God came to earth as a human.

When I asked if Christ would come and visit our home to see our tree before Christmas day, my mother must have realized that I had not understood her. It seemed natural to me at the time that this major effort to celebrate a birthday should not be missed by the person having the birthday. I liked the idea of having a birthday tree but was further confused when my mother told me that the Christmas tree would not be put up for my birthday in March.

She led me to the living room window and pointed to the stars and explained that Christ had died and gone to his father in the sky. This explanation made me curious as to the nature of God and I pondered the theme, as best a child could, while playing with the little statues, occasionally biting off the head of a lamb or shepherd when my mother wasn't watching.

Little did I know then that the lovely statue of Mary, mother of Jesus in the blue and white dress, would soon come to life for me on the Easter weekend that followed.

An Easter story

I remember being taken to the doctor various times that winter of 1945, because I had not been well. But on each trip the family doctor found nothing unusual.

It was not until Good Friday, a week after my fourth birthday, that I began to have severe pains in my stomach and complained to my mother. She tucked me under a blanket on the large living room sofa and went into our big country kitchen to serve dinner to my father and older sister.

I could hear them talking as I lay looking at the ceiling, but soon I heard a unique sound coming from the second floor. It was not footsteps but rather the swishing sound of silk or satin fabric rubbing against itself. I thought there must be a person upstairs who was about to come down the stairs.

From my location on the sofa I watched in anticipation for someone to appear. As the measured cadence of swishing fabric became louder, I wondered who it was. My parents had said nothing of a visitor in the house. Yet, someone was about to descend the stairs.

Then at the top step I saw a white slipper, shimmering like silk. Around it came a dress of the same white silk. Step by measured step, the flowing gown descended the stairs until I could see to the waist of this mystery person. At that point, a young lady bent forward to look me in the eye. She knew exactly where I was located in the room since her gaze focused directly upon me without the least hesitation. With a warm, friendly smile she continued down the stairs. Confident of her step, she locked her gaze on me alone.

I became fascinated with the clothing she wore. My first thought was that it was so different from that of my mother or her friends. As I gazed at the blue veil draped over her head, flowing down her white dress, I realized that this lady was an exact replica of the Christmas statue of Mary, identical in every way.

As she crossed the living room toward me, I began to sense that she was not an ordinary house guest but the *real* Mary, mother of the Christ child, the baby Jesus of the Christmas decorations.

She knelt beside me and asked, "Why are you so sad?"

I was thinking about all the things I could say, when she replied that she understood. I realized that she could hear my thoughts, and she told me I could hear hers.

She immediately proceeded to say that I was in grave danger. I was told that I must visit the doctor before the night was over or it would be too late, and then she would have to return for me. She asked if I understood what this meant.

I understood that I would not be able to come home again. She confirmed that I was correct. She then told me that I had a choice whether to stay or to leave with her. The choice was totally mine. To me she was so beautiful, so loving and understanding that, after only a moment's thought, I declared my intention to go with her.

She laughed softly and explained that my parents and sister loved me, and they would be very sad to have me taken away. I nevertheless persisted in my intention to go with her later that night. I noted something like frustration on her part at my decision. Her eyes turned toward the ceiling, and she was quiet for a moment. As she looked back down toward me her expression appeared more serious.

She said, "I am going to tell you a secret that few now know. If you stay with your family, you will see the Christ because he will come to live with the people of the world."

I understood clearly that the Christ would be walking among us again and not up in the stars as my mother had informed me at Christmas. I was excited and attempted to sit up as I asked, "When, when will he come?"

Again she laughed and carefully pushed me back down on my pillow and said, "You must remain still." She told me that I would be older, an adult perhaps, but he would come and I would be one of the first to see him and recognize him.

Although beyond my immediate understanding, I sensed that my life ahead could be wonderfully interesting.

Her more urgent task with me now began. She explained that I had to go to the hospital as soon as possible. I would have to convince my parents that it was an emergency. I knew the doctor and his office in the town but nothing about a hospital. She, knowing that my childish vocabulary was limited, told me exactly what to say to my parents and, in addition, what they would say to me. For each of their statements concerning the hospital, she had a ready reply, which I had to memorize. I had to repeat each sentence to her three times.

Eventually she appeared satisfied that I was prepared for my encounter with my parents. She also promised to have the family doctor ready and waiting for me at the hospital and made it clear that I should have no fear, all would be well. She then kissed my forehead and pulled the blanket up around my neck, reminding me to stay warm.

When departing, she passed the open doorway of the kitchen where the family was now eating. Yet, they did not notice her nor did she look at them. She approached the heavy green curtains that closed off the living room from the adjacent room and quietly melted into the fabric without disturbing them in the least. When I saw her vanish, even as a child of four, I knew she was extraordinary.

The moment she was gone I screamed for my parents. It was already dark outside and not much time remained to save myself. I had to get to the hospital as soon as possible.

When I told my parents, they repeated the same sentences Mary said they would. In fact, it was like living the experience twice. My father finally agreed to call the doctor at his office, even though it was late on Good Friday and almost everything in our small town had been closed since noon.

Much to my father's surprise, the doctor was in and requested that we go directly to the hospital. My swollen appendix was removed just as it was about to rupture. I remembered nothing until I awoke at the first sign of light on Easter Sunday morning.

A promise remembered

As the years passed, those memories faded and the entire event was pushed to the back of my mind. However, in 1982 a national television show from Hollywood suddenly brought them all back. What had started at Christmas so long ago was about to resume. As the memories flooded into my mind with great clarity, I remember thinking, "This could be what the Madonna promised in 1945."

Chapter 2

ॐ Coincidence and opportunity ॐ

"Life is what happens to us while we are making other plans."
—Thomas La Mance

After my life-saving encounter with the Madonna, I returned to being an ordinary kid growing up in a pleasant Midwestern town.

When I was 12 or 13, I read a book about a diplomat serving the Pharaoh of Egypt. This diplomat and his family were sent to live in a country often at war with Egypt, and so his life was very difficult and demanding of great patience. He and his family accepted these difficulties because they believed it was the only way to prevent further war and mistrust between the two countries.

I was fascinated with this fictional ancient story and decided that I, too, wanted to serve my country in such a capacity. But childhood dreams don't always manifest in the real world and, as I grew older, I realized my career ideal would be difficult to achieve. Nevertheless, when I enrolled at the University of Wisconsin in Madison, I decided to major in international relations and foreign languages, subjects I believed would prove useful if I ever did become a career diplomat.

As I was approaching the completion of my studies at the university in 1964, I realized I had not given much thought to life after graduation and had no idea what job opportunities might be available. I had retained my strong desire to do something overseas, more specifically in Brazil. I had studied Brazilian Portuguese and felt prepared to experiment with working for American interests in that country. I kept waiting for an opportunity to present itself, but nothing happened until just before graduation.

I completed one of my class exams early that day and headed for the student union for a snack. As I entered the building I noticed a group of people setting up an exhibit for the Peace Corps. Having no specific interest in the Peace Corps, I continued on my way past the exhibit when I heard a voice calling after me. A well-dressed gentleman in a dark suit and proper tie was shouting something to me about joining the Peace Corps and the great opportunities that awaited me.

I walked back to the table and we discussed my qualifications for overseas work, which seemed to impress him since he kept insisting this was exactly what I needed to prepare for my future. I told him that my major reservation about Peace Corps work was the lack of freedom to choose the country where you will serve.

"Not a problem," the man cheerfully answered. "We can make an exception for you."

Fine, I thought, but I also wanted to be doing something truly worthwhile and not just make friends and participate in nice activities, which may be useful at some level but really do little for the people living in poverty. I wanted a program that would be significant or lasting.

The recruiter insisted there was an important dimension to the Peace Corps that most people did not realize. He explained that American volunteers overseas gain much-needed practical knowledge of the world which is greatly lacking today in the United States government, schools and society in general. He suggested that the knowledge I would gain might one day pave the way for future opportunities in government or even the U.S. Foreign Service. My background, he continued, was perfect for such activities and, with the right attitude, I could create projects overseas which would be meaningful and long-lasting.

We negotiated further and, getting into the spirit of things, I fine-tuned my request to include specific regions of Brazil. This, too, could be arranged for me. Finally, I told him if he could make those exceptions for me, I would be willing to go to Brazil. But first I wanted to know on what authority he could make such promises.

"Pardon me," he said, "I have failed to introduce myself. I am David Rockefeller, a friend of the Peace Corps director in Washington."

For want of something to say, I told him he had the same name as the president of the Chase Manhattan Bank in New York.

"That's me," he said frankly. He explained that he believed so strongly in the Peace Corps and its ideals of helping others less fortunate, that he had called his old friend Sargent Shriver (the first Peace Corps director) and volunteered one day each year to recruit volunteers. Shriver suggested he come to the University of Wisconsin because of its excellent program in international relations and also because it had provided the largest number of volunteers in the previous year. So, today was Mr. Rockefeller's day, and I was his first candidate to accept a position.

Within weeks I was in a Peace Corps training program for volunteers assigned to Brazil. Within a few months I took my maiden voyage from New York to Rio de Janeiro. Mr. Rockefeller kept his promises to me, and I believe I fulfilled his vision of what a young American could do with the opportunity the Peace Corps offered.

Rio, the heart of Brazil

Arriving in Brazil was a dream come true, and our little band of eager new recruits went on a short but thrilling adventure for the first few weeks as we acclimatized in Rio. Lodging together in a small hotel near the center of Rio's commercial district, we took off in small groups each day to explore this exotic, tropical city—the 'heart of Brazil'—as Brazilians refer to their beloved capital. (This was 1964, and Rio was still the functioning capital.) Among our group, I was one of the few who spoke fluent Portuguese, the language we would need every day to survive. My years of advanced Brazilian Portuguese classes and studies of Brazilian history and geography would now give me a real edge.

Coming as I did from cold Wisconsin, this new tropical land of endless summers, endless fruit displays, and endless politeness from the Brazilians seemed like paradise. I knew, however, that beyond the big city excitement, as we went off to our distant corners of Brazil, we would soon come face to face with another, less glamorous world.

Most of my group was sent to Matto Grosso, a jungle state in transition near the Bolivian border. It was Brazil's frontier. I alone was sent to the Northeast coast to the city of Maceio, the capital of the state of Alagoas. This was a region of Brazil that was settled early by Portuguese explorers and had a long history of European culture.

Along with a group of American volunteers who had arrived earlier, my first assignment was to work with the health clinics scattered throughout the state. We were prepared to teach about preventable diseases from bad water and poor hygiene, but certainly not equipped to deal with the major illnesses these people were experiencing. A doctor visited each clinic only a few hours per week. So, when the doctor was not in, the public would not come, the clinic stood empty, and our work was almost non-existent.

I soon found more useful interests to fill my time. I moved into a shanty-town with a Peace Corps friend. All the houses in this slum were built of mud and had thatched roofs. We had one of the better 'models' with a concrete floor, tile roof, plaster over the mud walls, and even a window. The house was never dark because light seeped in through all the cracks in the tile roof. There was no indoor plumbing, running water, or beds. We slept in hammocks, as did many poor Brazilians.

My American housemate had a project working with the state government looking for water wells. I initiated a community effort to bring some structure to this collection of homes. Although there were hundreds of these dwellings, they were considered illegal squatters and, therefore, given no public services or utilities.

Through public meetings we encouraged residents to organize and press the government for electricity and water. This resulted in encouraging promises from politicians. The local Catholic priest agreed to help make further political contacts and also put me in contact with an American visitor from a Catholic aid organization in the U.S. This group offered funds to initiate the building of proper outdoor plumbing units throughout the community if, and only if, I would control the funds and oversee the construction. It was something the Peace Corps had trained me to do, so I gladly accepted the assistance.

I could not imagine the regional Peace Corps director would have any problem with this generous arrangement. So upon her return to Maceio, I sought her approval for this new opportunity. She was immediately opposed to the idea because of the financial links to the American aid organization. It was my first lesson in real-world politics. It seemed there were political taboos even in the Peace Corps.

I could only think of the progress we had already made in that slum community and desperately hoped this new project would further energize everyone involved. But I saw my plans evaporating, as the regional director would simply not allow my participation. It was unbelievable to me that the Peace Corps would deny these disenfranchised people, living in absolute poverty, this help for their most basic needs—toilets—because the funding would come from *our own country*. Surely, I reasoned, if I could just speak to the head Peace Corps director in Rio all would be well.

My conversations with the regional director only became more embittered in the following days. She rudely told me that, in her opinion, university political science majors such as myself were always trouble in the Peace Corps. She also accused me of having too many middle-class Brazilian friends, even though I spent my days with the poorest of the poor. I assumed she was referring to my teaching English at night to a group of journalists and university students. When I could see no further use in debating this issue with her, I arranged to go to Rio where, I assumed, the 'home office' would see my work differently.

I said good-bye to my many new Brazilian friends and appreciated their warm farewells that included articles in the newspaper about my service to their city. These positive stories had been written by the journalists from my English class.

My arrival in Rio, however, was not so pleasant. I was surprised when the Peace Corps director for the entire country (the country director) would not even give me an appointment to discuss the project. After a few weeks of filling in time by helping the office staff at headquarters, I became disillusioned with the whole organization. I wrote a letter to my parents in Wisconsin, outlining my dilemma and enclosing the newspaper articles from Maceio. I made it clear I was seriously thinking of returning home now, well before the end of my tour. It was then, when things appeared the darkest to me, that fate was designing other opportunities for my work in Brazil.

A *new opportunity*

During that first week back in Rio, I had met with an assistant to the director, whose job was to seek out new projects for the volunteers. He told me about some businessmen in South Central Brazil who had asked for a Peace Corps volunteer to help them establish a means of humanely dealing with the beggars on their city streets. He told me my language skills would be perfect for this project. It would also be in an area of the country where no volunteer had ever been placed, and I would have to work alone and without supervision. I thought this was too good to be true, and it was! The country director promptly rejected the idea, even though it was his own assistant who had proposed it. He would not even speak to me about his reasons and let his staff know he was hoping I would just go home.

Then one morning he walked into the office and called my name with great enthusiasm, "Wayne, come in and talk to me. We never did get an opportunity to chat."

The entire office staff looked up in amazement, as they knew this man had constantly refused to discuss with me the project in Northern Brazil or any other topic for that matter. Suddenly, for whatever reason, today was different. He ushered me into his office and proceeded to tell me that he had sent his deputy to Maceio to investigate my case. The report showed that I was never a troublemaker, as the regional director had claimed. "What do you want to do now," he asked.

I had only one thought on my mind, and that was the new project he had just disapproved, the 'beggar project'.

"No, no, not that," he yelled, when I told him.

Instead, he offered me a job in Rio de Janeiro, which I knew would be a do-nothing sort of task. He encouraged me to stay in Rio where I could enjoy the big-city life until my tour of duty was over. I also understood it was his way of saying, "Stay out of my way". Clearly, he wanted me somewhere he considered safe, where he could keep an eye on my activities. I remained adamant; I wanted nothing but the beggar project. Finally he relented but only after expressing his distaste for the project. He informed me that I would never hear from his office and not to expect any help. I would be completely on my own. I accepted on the spot.

Intervention from Washington

But why, I still wondered, had this man suddenly agreed to see me and then allow me the freedom to work in Southern Brazil, which was clearly against his wishes. I got my answer a week later in a letter from my mother.

It just so happened that our congressman, Melvin Laird (soon to become the secretary of defense) and a few aides from Washington were visiting my parents on the day my discouraging letter arrived. It may have been the only time Congressman Laird ever came to our home. As Laird discussed the new congressional district boundaries with my father, my mother went to the mailbox, where she found my letter and the newspaper clippings. She immediately showed them to the congressman, who became incensed that I had been treated so badly.

Apparently he had been a strong supporter of the Peace Corps concept from the moment it was proposed by President Kennedy. Laird now wanted to make it clear to Peace Corps-Washington that I should be allowed to work on any project I desired. Suddenly, I understood the country director's change of attitude toward me. It appeared that Washington congressional action was faster than international mail.

Although I never did know what Congressman Laird said to the Peace Corps director in Washington, I reasoned it was a powerful message, considering what happened during my first week in the town of my new assignment with the beggar project. I was living with a Brazilian family with four children in the town of Itapira, when I received a telegram from Peace Corps headquarters in Washington. I was aware that on that exact day Mr. Shriver had retired as the first director and was replaced by Mr. Vaughn.

I opened the telegram and read its short, terse message aloud: "Dear Mr. Peterson. I am the new director of the Peace Corps, *not* you." It was signed, "Jack Hood Vaughn, Peace Corps Director."

My new Brazilian family enjoyed the humor in the message.

Beggars everywhere

I spent my first weeks in the town of Itapira meeting with people who could help initiate a program for the street beggars. We opened an office in donated space on a quiet street, and I spoke at local business clubs asking for their support. We also discussed options with local government officials.

Eventually we organized sufficient volunteers to start documenting what the beggars needed and who, beyond the beggars, required assistance with food, housing or medical care. Having a clearer picture of the need, we then asked for donations of both food and money. We all agreed it was crucial that no funds should be accepted from the state or federal governments. Corruption was the rule in big government, and we wanted people to know that everything they donated was needed immediately and nothing would go to waste.

In those days in Brazil, as in many developing countries, people believed only the government should fund social projects. If the government is involved in any way, no private funds would even be forthcoming. We wanted people to understand that this was a new approach to solving their most basic social problem, caring for the poor and destitute. We made it known that whatever they donated would be used only in *their* town and channeled through *their* volunteer citizens. Much to everyone's surprise, donations came in faster than expected. People wanted to help, but previously had no way to donate with the exception of tossing coins to nameless beggars.

We discovered that many needy families refused to beg in public. They were too proud and would rather go hungry. This problem was resolved when people were given the option of coming into our office, called S.O.S., and speaking with a volunteer counselor privately, with dignity.

Since health and child care education was also a priority, we needed more volunteers. I first asked the most prestigious women in the community to serve as teachers on child care. I knew if they would volunteer, others would also join. At first they resisted, thinking they had too little to offer. But after their first lecture these ladies became aware of the overwhelming need. They were shocked that so many of these young mothers from impoverished families had little knowledge about the basics of caring for their babies: holding, feeding, washing, and preventing disease. Suddenly the rich ladies felt a new obligation to serve their community. They were also thrilled to find out how much they really knew.

Once each week, the poor women coming to the office to pick up food were required to attend a one-hour lecture on health or child care. Almost immediately, the streets of Itapira were free of beggars. We were confident that not a single person was going hungry. Most important, we knew the community had the will and ability to continue the program.

It was obvious that this volunteer method of dealing with beggars had the potential to be implemented in any town in Brazil. So I began a campaign of traveling with my two new Brazilian friends from Itapira to other nearby towns to tell them of our success. Our meetings, always well attended, were arranged by the local business clubs. Many came because they wanted to see who this American was with a social welfare message.

Soon we had other cities in the region starting their own S.O.S. operations. S.O.S. in Brazil means HELP, just as it does in the U.S. Translated from Portuguese, it means a Society of Social Works (Obras). We also received requests from mayors and church leaders to come and speak to their communities.

One day an officer from the Brazilian military headquarters in Rio arrived and asked if he could write a story about S.O.S. He took my photo and said we would be hearing from him again. Indeed we did, and again the direction of my life changed.

One Sunday, my Brazilian family presented me with the newspaper from Sao Paulo, Brazil's largest city and the current capital. The Sunday edition is also distributed to hundreds of other Brazilian cities. There on the front page was my picture and the story of S.O.S. The military man had given his story to the press. The photo was huge, with a headline about a Peace Corps volunteer helping to found a social welfare program with great success. The accompanying story transformed my project from a regional experiment into a nationally-recognized institution. The wife of the Brazilian president later became the official head of S.O.S., and the concept spread to cities throughout the country.

The article also affected me directly and immediately. The American consulate in Sao Paulo asked me to come for a meeting with the consul general. Two Brazilian friends went with me to that meeting. We were surprised when the American embassy asked if more Peace Corps volunteers could be useful to promote S.O.S. This was surely a change of heart. I remembered only too well the attitude the Peace Corps country director had when I departed to begin this project in Itapira.

When the American ambassador in Rio saw the newspaper story, he was pleased that the Peace Corps was finally receiving some positive press coverage in Brazil. I was told that he excitedly called the Peace Corps director to get more details. Unfortunately, the director had not even seen the paper and admitted he had no idea what I was doing in Itapira. Frustrated by this new development, he swallowed his pride and invited me to Rio for consultations.

In the meantime, embassy diplomats were visiting my little town to admire the project and to suggest that I stay on for another year as a volunteer. They believed the project was too important to leave to others in its initial stages of development. I, however, had no intention of extending my tour of duty in the Peace Corps and let that be known immediately.

So the diplomats suggested I become a career foreign service officer and request a diplomatic position at the American embassy in Brazil. This appealed to me, but I had no idea how long the process would take or if I would even be selected. The diplomatic service at that time had tens of thousands of applicants for only a dozen positions each year. I knew it would be very difficult.

"Not to worry," said my new diplomatic friends. "We will ask Washington to place you in the finals, which involves only an oral exam."

Eventually I was called into the embassy and sat before a group of officials who administered the oral exam. Thus, I completed my exams for the U.S. Foreign Service in Brazil even before departing the Peace Corps. Within weeks, I was notified that I had been accepted and would be posted back to Brazil as an assistant cultural attaché.

During my final months with the Peace Corps in Brazil, the director in Rio was desperately trying to catch up with the progress being made by our expanding S.O.S. offices. The Peace Corps was now begging for a larger role. The American ambassador to Brazil was demanding that more volunteers be placed with this popular new program, but he soon became disenchanted with the Peace Corps director and informed the State Department accordingly. Not surprisingly, Washington responded by asking the director to resign.

Perhaps in frustration, the country director invited me to Thanksgiving dinner. I tried to decline, saying I was too busy to make the long trip, but he demanded I come to Rio. I arrived for the afternoon dinner and found the American ambassador, Bobby and Ethel Kennedy among the guests. Kennedy was in Brazil to remind people that it was his brother John who, while president, had initiated the Alliance for Progress that benefited Latin American countries. Bobby was about to begin his own campaign for the U.S. presidency. I was seated next to Ethel and realized I was the only volunteer present. Although I enjoyed the opportunity to meet these exceptional people, I wondered, "Why me?"

It became clear after the Kennedys and the ambassador departed. The Peace Corps director took me aside and accused me of sabotaging his position in Rio and his future in the diplomatic service. He wanted answers and probably hoped I could help salvage his career. At this point, I'm sure he regretted his earlier decision to cut off communication with me. I tried in vain to convince him I had not been asking officials in Washington to remove him. It had been the ambassador who was displeased with his performance. I had not said a bad word about him but neither had I lied to the embassy about his refusing me any support or contact when I began the S.O.S project.

I went back to the project in Itapira for another few months to peacefully work until the end of my tour of duty as a volunteer. Several times over the past 30 years I have returned to that town and renewed my friendship with those I consider to be some of the most gracious and thoughtful people I have ever known.

I had only a few weeks at home in Wisconsin before I was due in Washington to be sworn into the foreign service and my new career.

Chapter 3

❧ Entering the halls of power ❧

"Life can only be understood backwards;
but it must be lived forwards."
— Soren Kierkegaard

It was early 1967 and I spent a few months in Washington training for work with the American embassy in Brazil. All went smoothly until our flight to Rio on Pan American Airways. I was traveling with two other junior foreign service officers who were also going to Brazil. Somewhere over the Caribbean between Miami and Panama, our 707 jet lost power in one engine. This was not a traumatic situation, as the pilot assured us we could easily make Panama, and we did. There the plane was repaired while we waited, but many of the passengers chose not to continue on with the flight to Bogota, Colombia.

Then, somewhere between Panama and Bogota, our plane lost power in *two* engines. We had a light load aboard and were relieved when the pilot again informed us all would be well. Indeed, the jet did make it up over the mountains to Bogota on the remaining two engines. It was the next leg to Lima, Peru where things got rough. I had a premonition about the flight when my two friends and I were the only passengers who would re-board the plane.

It was already dark when we departed Bogota. After some time in flight I told my companions it seemed strange that the flaps on the wing on our side were in the down position, as if for landing. I also noticed that the plane was rolling back and forth. I was told not to worry, but almost immediately the captain called all the crew up front for a meeting that seemed to last for a very long time. I had a very bad feeling when the meeting broke up and the cabin attendants ran past us in tears and hid in the far back of the plane. I knew this could not be good news. However, not a single crew member came and talked to us about any problem.

Eventually I went to the back and found the attendants lying on the floor with blankets over their heads. I innocently asked if they would be serving drinks or food.

One young woman appeared from beneath her blanket long enough to inform me that anything on the plane was mine for the taking.

"Free?" I asked.

There was no reply.

I helped myself to a few small bottles of liquor and went back to my seat. I poured my friends a drink and we discussed the strange attitude of the crew. A few minutes later the captain himself came back and asked how we were doing. We asked if there was anything wrong.

"My God," he said, "hasn't the cabin crew informed you?"

We sat there shaking our heads "no".

He proceeded to say, "I don't think we are going to make it."

"Make it where?" I asked.

Now *he* was shaking his head "no".

The gravity of our situation was becoming clear. Eventually the pilot told us we had been flying on two engines and now the third had stopped. We were left with a single engine on the far outer end of one wing. Trying to make my friends feel more comfortable, I suggested that, as long as we were doing so well on one engine and the airport in Lima is at sea level, all we had to do was slowly descend.

The pilot kept shaking his head "no". He explained that the one working engine was not designed to run at full throttle for more than a few minutes. Without full throttle the plane would crash, and with it the engine would either explode or disintegrate. He suggested that could happen at any minute.

My last question to him was, "Can't we glide just enough to land in the ocean safely?"

With a very sober, pale face he said we would glide no better than a rock.

I could see he was not trying to be funny. The three of us quickly had another drink.

After that, every minute seemed an eternity. Here I was, en route to my very first assignment as a foreign service officer, and I was about to crash land in some South American jungle. Not a good way to begin and end a career—all at the same time.

Whether by luck, fate or divine intervention, the plane *did* make it to Lima intact, but not without further drama. As we approached the airport, the plane was hanging to one side, and I feared the powerless wing would hit the ground first and spin us into a deadly crash.

Just as we cruised over the first patch of asphalt—still almost 30 feet above the ground—the remaining engine died. After a moment of absolute silence, the plane dropped onto the runway like a rock. Tires exploded, and the powerless plane silently swerved from one direction to another, all the while being pursued by every fire engine in Lima. We went from Tarmac to dirt and back again several times, finally coming to a safe stop. We three passengers were rushed out the door and down a stairway that had been pushed against the plane by firemen. It was a scene straight out of a Hollywood disaster movie.

Having landed safely, if not a little shaken and slightly drunk, we were met by an American embassy official in Lima. Before we had a chance to explain our traumatic experiences, we were criticized for being late and missing our official party at the embassy. We were so happy to be alive that we did nothing official on our two days in Lima. Then we continued our journey to Rio de Janeiro and were met by more sympathetic embassy officials.

A career begins in Rio

The career of a foreign service officer with the U.S. Government is very different from any other job in government or in the business world. Those who are assigned as diplomats are much like the men of the Renaissance in Western Europe. They are expected to have sufficient knowledge to do a wide variety of jobs depending upon the needs of the moment. Within the foreign service there are numerous titles, some official, such as 'secretary of the embassy', and some working titles, such as 'cultural attaché', 'political attaché', 'public affairs officer', which more precisely describe the nature of one's assignment. The term 'diplomat' may be applied to any of these titles and indicates a certain rank within the foreign service. Throughout my foreign service career I held a number of these titles, beginning with cultural attaché.

A cultural attaché's job is to represent American cultural interests in a foreign country, and it covers a wide range of activities. Unlike the task of a political attaché, it does not involve reporting events in the political life of a foreign country to Washington.

I considered my job far more interesting, as my task was to educate Brazilian leaders and elite members of society about American culture, which included our political interests. At times my job involved being an escort to visiting American entertainers, giving seminars at universities, promoting American interests on radio and television, and writing articles for newspapers. It also involved the administration of international programs, such as the Fulbright Scholarship Program, and attending frequent meetings and receptions at the request of the host government and various special-interest groups.

I spent five years in Brazil working with cultural programs for the American embassy. Because I spoke Portuguese better than many of the others at the embassy, I was often required to give public lectures, do TV shows, and cut ribbons at official ceremonies sponsored by Brazilian organizations. It was an extremely interesting job, allowing me to meet many creative people, not only Brazilians but visiting American dignitaries as well. No two days were ever the same. I remember vividly my assignment of escorting boxer Mohammed Ali around Sao Paulo.

One day when we had some free time, I asked Mohammed if he wanted to meet Johnny Mathis, who was on a singing tour in Brazil. Neither of us had met Mathis before, but with my embassy connections these things could be easily arranged. It turned out to be an interesting mix of personalities and professions. The three of us got on well together. In my view, this may be the most important work that diplomats do: facilitating communications between peoples of different cultures and backgrounds.

Moving on to Asia

After my tour of duty in Brazil was over, I had options to be assigned to any one of several embassies in Southeast Asia. I had hoped to be posted to Thailand. In preparation I entered the Asian Studies training program in Washington. Realizing I would be in a predominantly Buddhist society for several years, I went looking for books to take with me to Asia. I found a good bookstore in Georgetown and was overwhelmed with the huge selection of books on Buddhist thought and culture. Not knowing where to begin, I asked the only person available.

He was a young man standing beside me, also looking at the Asian culture books. I asked if he knew something of this topic and, if so, could he possibly advise me. He smiled and, in a very matter-of-fact manner, told me he was the perfect person to have asked, as he was a student and scholar of Buddhist knowledge both East and West. Then, without hesitation, he knelt down and retrieved from the bottom shelf a small book called the *Diamond Sutra*. He pointed out that this book was not carried in most bookshops and I was fortunate that this particular bookstore would have such an esoteric work.

"Fine," I said. "What else do you recommend?"

"Nothing more," he insisted.

I explained that I was going to be in Asia for two years and needed lots of Buddhist material to study.

"No," he replied. "This is all you will need."

Seeing my puzzlement he added, "If you can read and understand this book in two years, you will be very successful in understanding the knowledge of the Buddha." He wished me well and departed.

I *did* read that book for two years and, with each reading, new ideas would form in my mind. I do not know, however, if I was successful in understanding everything the book hoped to impart to the reader.

My destination to Asia is changed

My plans for Asia were suddenly changed. This is not unusual in the diplomatic service. I know of many officers who were boarding flights for their new assignment when they were called off the plane because the country of assignment was suddenly changed.

I had only a few days warning that my own destination was being changed. Henry Kissinger, the secretary of state, had just announced that a cease-fire agreement would be signed with the North Vietnamese in Paris. The United Nations would establish a peace-keeping unit in South Vietnam, and the American military had only a few weeks to depart. I was assigned to Vietnam as a special officer with the American embassy to follow the activities of the United Nations peace-keeping units in that country.

I arrived in Saigon on January 27, 1973, the day the agreement was signed in Paris. This will forever be imprinted on my mind, for within a week I was asked by the American ambassador to escort back to San Francisco the first American prisoner of war released by the North Vietnamese. It was a wild experience crossing the Pacific with calls coming to me in the cockpit of the aircraft from the secretary of state in Washington. He knew the American press was going to turn this into a national media event and he was, understandably, concerned that a junior officer was in charge of the situation.

In San Francisco I was told there were hundreds of members of the press corps as well as TV and radio crews waiting at the airport. The F.B.I., acting on instructions from Washington, insisted I depart the plane through the cockpit window to avoid the press. I soon discovered how high the cockpit of a 747 jetliner is off the ground and had serious reservations about the plan. However, several F.B.I. agents managed to stuff me through a very small window, and down a long ladder I descended, as other agents waited below. My baggage was tossed out after me. It was just another job for the 'Renaissance man'.

Before returning to Saigon I stayed over in San Francisco for several days of rest. Although the Paris cease-fire treaty was never implemented, my tour of duty at the American embassy was relatively peaceful. For several months I and several other diplomats visited many regions of South Vietnam. This surprised the local people, as they had been told that all the Americans were gone. The military had indeed departed very rapidly, but the Vietnamese did not really understand what an embassy official did in their country. They may have thought we were disguised military men.

The end was near

A few months later I was appointed the American consul for Nha-Tran. My assignment was to open a public affairs office at the American consulate general in Nha-Tran and act as liaison to the Vietnamese military and civilian leaders. Nha-Tran had been a popular beach resort with the former French colonialists and was still a beautiful place when I arrived.

It soon became obvious to me that, even with the enactment of a cease-fire, the end was near for the South Vietnamese. Without the Americans, the Vietnamese leaders appeared to be resigned to inevitable defeat.

Even with my work, I had time to explore the country and came to appreciate the ancient culture of Vietnam and was charmed by its art and artists. During my travels across Vietnam, Laos, Thailand, and several other Southeast Asian countries, I always attempted to learn about the culture, visit the old palaces and temples, and seek out those who would tell me about their society.

In Saigon I visited the home of a Buddhist film maker and part-time dealer in antique Chinese porcelains and a few other art objects. I admired a beautiful, 500-year-old statue of Maitreya Buddha and asked if it were for sale. He responded that, over the years, many Americans at the embassy had attempted to purchase this statue, but he would not release it for sale because it was a sacred object. He made it clear that the statue needed to be not only in the care of a Buddhist, but also with a person who would respect its sacred nature. Time passed, and on occasion I purchased a few Chinese porcelains from this man. Then one day my embassy colleague informed me that the antique dealer wanted to see me again. He believed the man was ready to sell the Maitreya Buddha statue—but only to me.

I eagerly returned to admire the exquisite red and gold statue. After much tea and food, I was again queried about my willingness to keep the statue sacred. There was, for example, a specific manner in which it had to be handled and, if I promised to cooperate, the statue would be mine. Of course I agreed and eventually took that statue with me to Africa and then back to Washington. I believe I have always managed to live up to the instructions of its former owner. Only many years later would I discover how truly important that statue would become to me. It was either a wonderful coincidence or a real miracle.

My work in Vietnam comes to a close

Time in Vietnam passed quickly for me. I departed the consulate in Nha-Tran for the last time and headed to Saigon for the return flight to Washington. During my first night back in Saigon, the Vietcong attacked Nha-Tran. Bombs exploded at the airfield I had departed only hours earlier. Only a few months later, the entire U.S. embassy presence in Vietnam would be gone. My personal household effects, including the Maitreya Buddha statue, were the last to escape Saigon before the end. Any Americans departing Saigon after me were forced to leave their possessions in Vietnam. Unlike too many of my countrymen, I returned from Vietnam safe and sound.

Out of Africa

When my superiors in Washington offered me several postings in Africa, I took the advice of other diplomats and selected the American embassy in Kenya. Upon my arrival in Nairobi I found the house where I wanted to live. Although it was beyond the housing budget limit of the embassy, they finally agreed to rent it for me. It had the most beautiful lawns surrounded by tropical flowers, vines and trees. A high fence and night guard kept out unwanted animals that might wander over from the nearby plains of the great Serengeti Game Park. After settling in, I asked the neighbors why this section of the city was called Karen. They said I was living on the former property of Baroness Karen Blixen, the woman whose life story became the basis for the book and film *Out of Africa*.

Kenya, I found, was a place where memorable events took place daily. I will never forget the game parks filled with animals, the rich tribal ceremonies, the British cultural activities in Nairobi, the splendid beaches around the port of Mombasa, the old coastal Portuguese forts, the Arab towns, and the mountains, both Mt. Kenya, directly on the equator, and Mt. Kilimanjaro, the highest point in Africa—both visible from the embassy office windows. In addition there were the absolutely splendid soda lakes on the floor of the Great Rift Valley, where each lake was covered with millions of pink flamingos. It was Africa at its best.

The mysterious Mikella

My last memorable experience in Kenya was not the scenery, but rather a meeting with an elderly, aristocratic British woman named Mikella, a long-time resident of Nairobi.

I first met Mikella at an embassy reception and was at once fascinated by her appearance. Overdone facial makeup, a wild hair color and good conversation were her trademarks. I was told that her first husband, an English Lord, was the last colonial English supreme court justice of the Sudan. She had built herself a castle in Nairobi and was beloved by Kenyans, including President Kenyatta.

The evening I first saw her, she entered the formal reception room and headed directly toward me. Without a word of introduction, she asked if I would be interested in attending her weekly séance. I was shocked, polite, curious and noncommittal.

After the reception, I asked another American diplomat if he knew Mikella. I was surprised that both he and the American ambassador were interested in Mikella and eager to attend her séances, but neither had ever been invited. Each day, I was told, dozens of Africans would come to sit on the lawn in front of her castle and wait, hoping to be seen and then blessed by Mikella. It was rumored that she had exceptional healing powers and could move objects simply with her mind. I would eventually experience these powers for myself.

The miracle cure

Near the end of my tour of duty in Nairobi I became very ill. For several months I was unable to walk or do any movement without extreme pain. Every joint in my body was swollen and stiff, and medicine provided no relief. I was first hospitalized and then sent to recover at the home of an embassy officer. When there were no signs of improvement, they arranged for me to fly back to Washington. An ambulance was to meet me at the plane and take me directly to the hospital. Naturally everyone feared for me flying such a distance in my condition. They knew it would be a gruesome experience. Then Mikella entered the picture.

An embassy official telephoned Mikella the day before I was scheduled to leave and asked her to come to my bedside and do a healing. Although she wanted to help, she explained that it was impossible because she was going to be married on the following day and was just too occupied. President Kenyatta had insisted her wedding be televised to the nation and this had placed additional burdens on her. But she generously offered another solution: I was to meditate at 7:30 that evening, and at the same time she would send me a healing from her home. I did my best to cooperate and then went directly to sleep.

I awoke the following morning dreading the trip back to Washington. Suddenly I realized I could move freely again. I got out of bed and walked without pain for the first time in several months. I could actually move my legs instead of doing a mini-shuffle step. I got dressed on my own and went downstairs, to the utter amazement of the household. I walked up the steps and into the huge 747 jetliner unassisted and, without any further problems, flew to Frankfort, Germany and then on to Washington.

The Washington ambulance crew was waiting to carry me off the plane. Instead they caught up with me walking through the airport carrying my own hand-bags and insisted I be wheeled away on their rolling cot to the ambulance. Maybe they thought they wouldn't be paid unless I cooperated. So, there I was, in the middle of that huge room at Dulles International Airport, taking off my jacket and being helped onto a gurney. After a day in the hospital, the doctors informed me they could find nothing unusual and I was free to go. I felt just fine!

A Washington career begins

After my hospital experience I was assigned to a Washington-based job for two years, which all American diplomats must do on a routine basis. It is absolutely necessary for foreign service personnel to re-familiarize themselves with American life between long periods of service abroad. I was sent to the policy office at the U.S. Information Agency. This office is in constant contact with our embassy officers overseas as well as the highest-ranking officials within the agency in Washington. For me, it was a perfect place to be.

After several years I was again offered an embassy position, this time in Buenos Aires, Argentina. For the first time in my career, I was not interested in going overseas. For some reason, I firmly believed that truly great events in the political and social life of the planet were going to take place in the near future. I was afraid that if I left Washington I would not be able to participate in these important changes. After all, Washington is the political capital of the world. I did not know exactly what these changes would be, but I was convinced they were about to take place soon.

So I refused the assignment in Argentina, which is not an option for diplomats, and was told to either accept it or resign. I resigned. Within one day I was hired back at the same agency as a director of the Fulbright Scholarship Program. It was a 'coincidence' that this agency was looking for someone at that very moment, and I walked in the door with all the qualifications they wanted—and more. Since the program was also partially administered by American diplomats overseas, I had the added advantage of making inspection trips to various parts of the world. That was the beginning of a civil service career that lasted until my retirement in 1997.

The Fulbright Scholarship is an international program, funded by Congress, which functions in over 150 foreign countries. Through the exchange of senior academics, the program hopes to make the world a safer and better place to live. Senator Fulbright, who sponsored the legislation to establish this program, knew all too well the follies of World War II. He believed we could eliminate such disasters in the future if nations learned to cooperate at the highest level through the exchange of ideas among intelligent people who had an understanding of each other's political, economic and cultural structures. In fact, many leaders in foreign countries over the past forty years have had a Fulbright experience.

Another new opportunity

It was just about the time I was settling into this great new job that I got the *real* message I had been waiting to hear. What I deeply sensed about impending, dramatic world changes suddenly became the topic on a popular TV talk show, and my life would never be the same.

Chapter 4

✂ A promise fulfilled ✄

"I belong to everyone.
I do not want you to accept or reject me.
It is your inner experience which counts.
Every individual will find
he can make his contribution to society."
—Maitreya

February 1982. It was Wednesday evening and a busy week was half over. I was happy just to flop in front of the television and flip through the channels. I paused on the "Merv Griffin Show" airing from Hollywood when I saw Merv holding up a book. It was the book's title that grabbed my attention—*The Reappearance of the Christ and the Masters of Wisdom.*

As usual when watching TV, my interest in something was interrupted by a commercial break. This provocative title, however, caused me to wait and see what discussion would take place afterwards. I thought it might be some fundamentalist Christian message, but could not imagine Merv Griffin promoting a religious group on prime time TV. Indeed the interview had nothing to do with a religious organization, and it was very exciting

Merv began by introducing Benjamin Creme from England as the author of this new book, *The Reappearance of the Christ and the Masters of Wisdom.* A second guest, Gore Vidal, had just completed his own book on a spiritual subject, *Creation.* The two authors were being interviewed together by Merv. I remember Vidal saying he did not think Creme's book would be a big seller in the U.S. because the content was too distant from traditional Christian ideas of the Christ.

Millions are introduced to 'Maitreya'

During this discussion, Creme said that the one Christians call the Christ had reappeared and was living in a major industrial city in the Western world. This time his name was Maitreya and he was bringing with him a large group of his disciples, highly advanced, spiritual men called the Masters of Wisdom. He said we could expect to hear more about Maitreya on local and international news programs very soon.

Maitreya's purpose, Creme indicated, was to help us realize our innate divinity through learning to live in right relationship as brothers and sisters of one great family. The first step was to establish sharing as the way to eliminate the poverty and starvation that caused millions around the world to die daily in the midst of plenty. Maitreya was emerging in time to help us save ourselves and the planet, and would make himself known to all in a televised 'Day of Declaration' soon to come.

As I was soaking in these brief statements, I was surprised to realize that, as a traditional Christian, I could easily accept the idea of a superhuman being named Maitreya as the reappeared Christ, or World Teacher. The idea of sharing the world's resources appealed to me, as well, for in my many years abroad I had seen the poverty and starvation he spoke of firsthand. As I viewed Creme on that television show, I knew in my heart that this was the message I had been waiting to hear since that initial reappearance message in 1945 from the Blessed Mother.

In fact, as strange as Creme's ideas may have been to most viewers, I not only accepted them easily but was eager to learn more. The vision of the Blessed Mother, which I had almost forgotten after so many years, was suddenly very fresh again in my mind. I was determined to explore this story from Benjamin Creme without delay. Could it be, I wondered, that the Christ is truly back walking in the streets of our cities just as the Madonna promised me? I just had to find the book and read it for myself. I felt it would either be so extraordinary that it would change my life or it would be a huge disappointment.

The book that changed my life

The morning following the TV show I spent considerable time on the telephone trying to find a bookstore in the metropolitan Washington area that had a copy of Benjamin Creme's book. Obviously, a few other people had the same idea since every bookstore I called claimed to have sold the last copy that morning. I waited several weeks for my copy to arrive by mail.

Eventually, I discovered that the esoteric information in Creme's book, although new to me, nevertheless rang true. Reading the chapters gave me the feeling that I had known this material before but had simply forgotten it. I knew that was not true, since I had not come in contact with esoteric literature until then, or even any new age writings. In spite of this, I felt the ideas presented by Benjamin Creme were logical and did not conflict with my own views.

Hierarchy of Masters

The Reappearance of the Christ and the Masters of Wisdom discussed in depth what I had heard briefly on TV. I was introduced to something called the Spiritual Hierarchy, the group of Masters with the Christ at its head, which oversees the development of all life on this planet. The Masters of Wisdom, I learned, are human beings as we are who are ahead of us in evolution. They have progressed through all the lessons that this planet can offer and no longer need human experience. For example, one of the Masters working with Maitreya now is the former apostle St. John the Beloved. Fortunately for humanity, the Masters choose to remain with us to guide and protect. This great sacrifice is part of their own spiritual evolution, about which we can know very little.

Spiritual Hierarchy and Masters of Wisdom are somewhat esoteric terms for the same great spiritual beings known by other names among different religions and cultures. Coming from a Christian background, one might call this group the Kingdom of God, and the Masters might be known to some as elder brothers, angels or, in some cases, saints. While the names may vary, the personages behind those names are one and the same—the Guardians of *all* humanity.

Through their disciples, who are men and women in the world, the Masters deal with every aspect of human endeavor. They are, for example, the inspirers of great scientific works, as well as high achievements in the creative arts. Their disciples, whom they mentally inspire, work in all fields including the political, medical, religious, educational and artistic. These men and women may or may not be aware that they are, in fact, disciples of the Masters.

The Hierarchy of Masters has been with us throughout the history of humanity, guiding, teaching and protecting us. At one time they were openly present. But for many thousands of years they have worked from behind the scenes, taking upon themselves the responsibility of overseeing our evolution from their hidden places in the world's deserts and high mountains.

Now, at the beginning of a new age, the Masters of Wisdom are returning slowly into our midst, in carefully measured steps, so they do not infringe our free will or create unnecessary fear. Soon they will live and work openly once again in the everyday world.

They know the plight of humanity and the solutions to our

problems. Very simply, the Masters respond to our cries for help. On a personal level, millions of people can attest to receiving such help in times of crisis from one of these great beings, which they might assume is an angel.[1] This relationship between the Masters and humanity will become increasingly evident as their gradual emergence takes place. Eventually, they will be able to answer many questions regarding our evolution and the spiritual path.

Who is Maitreya?

As I read Creme's book, I learned more about the Christ, or World Teacher, whose personal name is Maitreya. He is the one awaited by all the major religions albeit unknown to them. The Christians wait for the return of the Christ, Buddhists for the next Buddha, Muslims for the Imam Mahdi, Hindus for a reincarnation of Krishna, and the Jews for the Messiah. These are all different names for one individual, Maitreya, who is here not as a religious leader but as a teacher for *all* humanity.

In *The Reappearance of the Christ and the Masters of Wisdom*, Benjamin Creme has this to say about Maitreya:

"We shall shortly realise that there lives among us now a man who embodies in Himself the hope and aspirations of the religious groups as well as the practical aspirations for a better life for all, of the political and economic thinkers.

"On July 19th 1977, this Great One, Maitreya, the Christ, the Lord of Love Himself, entered His 'point of focus' as it is called, a certain country in the modern world.

"He will show humanity the steps which it should take to regenerate itself, and to create a civilisation based on sharing, co-operation and goodwill, leading inevitably to world brotherhood.

"Soon we shall see this man of extraordinary qualities. Recognise Him by His spiritual potency; His wisdom and breadth of view; His inclusiveness and love; His grasp of human problems and ability to indicate the solutions to man's dilemma—political and economic, religious and social.

"He is Divine, having perfected Himself and manifested the Divinity potential in each of us. He is a man too, and comes as a brother, teacher and friend, to inspire humanity to create for itself a better and happier world. To those who can respond He will show the way into that state of Being in which Reality, or God, is an ever-present experience, and of which joy and love are the expression."

The esoteric teachings say that Maitreya will be with us until the end of the age of Aquarius, more than 2,000 years from now.

Maitreya himself has said:

"I am indeed among you, in a new way: your brothers and sisters know me, have seen me and call me friend and brother."

"My plan is to reveal myself stage by stage, and to draw together around me those enlightened souls through whom I may work. This process has begun, and soon, in my center, my presence will become known."

I visit the local Theosophical Society

Having studied the book I felt there was no way to proceed with this information, except to wait for Maitreya to appear publicly and the Day of Declaration. But I couldn't sit still. I made a visit to the Washington, DC Theosophical Society.

I had only learned of the society by reading Creme's book and was surprised to find a branch so close to me. I reasoned that among this group perhaps there would be others interested in the story of Maitreya. It was the only organization I could think of where I could expect to find people with an understanding of

Masters and who would recognize the name Maitreya.

The Theosophical Society was located in a residential area on the north side of the city near the Maryland state line. It was an ordinary looking house, like all the others on this quiet tree-lined street. Children were playing in the street when I arrived. Inside I met a woman who knew that Benjamin Creme was coming to Washington the following week to give a lecture. This was exciting news. I could hardly believe my good fortune.

I was told by this good Theosophist that others in the society were not interested in Benjamin Creme and his story, but her good friend, a Mrs. Bamah Ferrara, held weekly gatherings of those who were. She told me to call for the particulars, which I promptly did.

Mrs. Ferrara also told me about Benjamin Creme's coming to town, not only for a lecture but a meditation. She invited me to the weekly meeting of her group where they did this new form of meditation which had been established through Creme by one of the Masters. Called Transmission Meditation, it was a service activity in which energy from the Masters was 'stepped down' by the meditators and made available to the world. In the process the meditators' own spiritual development was enhanced manifold. I understood that it was another way to help Maitreya and the Masters emerge as soon as possible.

Here was a good channel for my new aspiration, even though I had never meditated in my life. It was also an opportunity to meet others who had an interest in the emergence of Maitreya. But what intrigued me the most was the coincidence of this meeting and Benjamin Creme's coming to Washington. If I had not gone to the Theosophical Society on that eventful Sunday, I never would have known about it and would never have experienced the extraordinary events of that weekend.

Creme's visit proved to be a real eye-opener and the beginning of my involvement with the reappearance. It was during his three-day visit that I became convinced the Masters spoken of in his book were indeed real and active in the world.

Chapter 5

✖ Getting my attention ✖

"My plans shall not fail.
My emergence takes place.
My gifts shall I bestow, my words shall guide.
My will shall strengthen.
My teachings shall show you the nature of God."
—Maitreya

During my first meeting with the Transmission Meditation group, it was confirmed that Benjamin Creme would be in town for three days. On the first day, the group would have a private meditation with him, and I was invited to join them. The next day was the public lecture, and the final day would be a public meditation.

As Creme's visit progressed, the story of the reappearance took on a new life for me. During each of the events I had an extraordinary personal experience. After these experiences I was absolutely sure Maitreya was the reappeared Christ, and his emergence into the everyday world of humanity was very real and probably not far away.

The private meditation with Creme and 40 others—only my second session—was again held at the home of Bamah Ferrara in suburban Maryland. It was a bright, sunny afternoon and people had gathered on the back lawn. With food, drink and time to chat beforehand, this was my best opportunity yet to meet so many people interested in Creme's story.

Initially, I had little idea of what they would be like. My concern was that I would encounter a religious cult or an organization with dogmatic demands. Therefore, I was relieved that the people I met came from a variety of religious and spiritual backgrounds. Many were Christians, some were Muslims, while others considered themselves new age spiritual people.

Most importantly, there was no organization, no dogma, no leaders, just people cooperating to bring Benjamin Creme's message to the public. The guests all appeared very normal and had ordinary occupations. This was not some cult, I realized, since they all freely expressed individual views of the spiritual life. There were no conditions or obligations; it was just a group of people coming together each week to meditate.

Day one: private Transmission Meditation

About 5:00 in the afternoon after our picnic, we went to a basement room for the Transmission Meditation. The previous session had lasted for one hour, so I assumed this one would be the same. I had little other expectation about what would follow.

After everyone was seated, Mr. Creme offered some comments about the importance of Transmission Meditation as a service to humanity. He explained that the energies from Hierarchy would ordinarily 'bounce' off of humanity but, directed through the group, would be stepped down into useable form. This was much like electricity being transmitted and transformed for safe use in our homes. In this stepped-down form the spiritual energy was more readily available to benefit humanity and the planet. When he was present at a meditation, Creme explained, he was 'overshadowed' mentally by Maitreya and, therefore, the group was overshadowed or touched directly by Maitreya's energy. Additionally, he said he would announce each shift in the qualities of the energy. He said the meditation would last until the energy stopped, but we were free to leave whenever we had to go.

The meditation begins

With the lights off we proceeded. What struck me was that moments before Creme would announce a new shift in the energy, I could feel it, and I was thinking, "This man is not joking about energy passing through our bodies—I can truly feel this happening."

Since I could confirm for myself that something he called energy was flowing through me, and presumably the group, I was satisfied that his statements were true.

The struggle begins

All went well for the first few minutes, but suddenly a very unpleasant feeling, something like an electric shock, passed through my body. Mr. Creme announced that we had just received the energy of power of the first ray, or the Father aspect of the Holy Trinity.

Whatever it was, it was so powerful I stopped breathing. Struggling to breathe, I discovered I couldn't move. Then, my heart seemed to stop. I thought, "If I don't get out of here, I'm going to die." But I was unable to communicate my problem to the people beside me!

In the midst of this panic I thought I heard someone say loudly, "Don't panic. You're leaning forward. Just lean back and slowly take in a breath of air, very slowly."

I realized, as I followed the instructions, that I could move, but still, I wanted to leave the room.

"You will be fine," said the voice that sounded very much like Creme's.

Again he instructed me to relax and to breathe in slowly and deeply. Gradually my panic subsided and I was breathing normally again.

Nevertheless, that forceful energy continued to pass through me to the extent that I was very uncomfortable and quite concerned about what it was doing to by body. I had visions of my death in Mrs. Ferrara's darkened basement. I could almost see the humorous newspaper headlines about a man being struck dead during meditation. Years after the event it is funny but, at the time, I was really fearful.

Again I was assured that all would be well if I just relaxed.

How did he know how I felt?

Only when I was feeling safe again did I recall that I had not spoken a word *out loud* about my struggle. It was dark and I was sitting along the same wall as Creme; he could not see me. Even if he had wanted to see me, I was out of his line of vision. Yet, I was sure that it was his voice and that he had known exactly what to say to me each time I had a specific thought. Somehow, I decided, he had become aware of the problems I was having, understood my panic completely and had responded to me with encouragement. Then it occurred to me that he must have been reading my thoughts.

I finally calmed down and continued to meditate. Milder energies flowed through me, and I had little awareness of what was going on around me as I focused on them.

Suddenly I heard Creme say, "That is it. It's over."

I opened my eyes and realized that the two of us were the only people remaining in the room. The meditation had lasted until 1:30 a.m. During those hours from late afternoon until 1:30 in the morning, the others had gone. I never heard them. I remembered only my initial panic, his voice calming me, and the energies that seemed to flow through me until it was over.

Day two: an apology to Mrs. Ferrara

The following day, before driving to Baltimore for Benjamin Creme's lecture, I visited Mrs. Ferrara at her home. Since she was the hostess of the previous night's program, I felt my apology for disrupting the group should go to her. I was truly embarrassed.

Her first comment was, "What are you talking about?"

I reviewed what had happened and how disturbed I was that Mr. Creme had to calm me down.

She said, "I don't know what you're talking about. I sat next to him and he said nothing to you about any problem."

I insisted that he spoke to me loudly and clearly in his distinct Scottish accent. I told her that he seemed to be reading my every thought and responding to each need.

Her suggestion was that I probably heard him telepathically.

At first I dismissed this possibility, but she insisted there had been no verbal conversation between Creme and me.

She assured me that none of the others heard a conversation and offered, "Let's call a few people and ask them." She connected with four or five who were unanimous. No audible conversation had taken place.

I slowly accepted the idea that, indeed, a two-way telepathic interchange must have occurred. How, I did not know. But there was no denying what I had felt and heard. The whole experience was real for me.

Creme's lecture that evening had another surprising confirmation in store for me.

Day two: the lecture

It was a very hot and humid summer night in Baltimore. Filled to capacity, the small auditorium felt stifling even with air conditioning. Latecomers had to stand.

Creme presented much of what I remembered from his book.

New to me was the impressive depth of his knowledge regarding international political and economic matters and the general problems facing humanity. He made it very clear that Maitreya was needed in the world to help us learn to live in right relationship.

Following the intermission Creme answered questions from the audience. The final question concerned the connection between Maitreya and a holy man in India named Sathya Sai Baba, who millions of followers worldwide believe to be God incarnate. Creme explained that Sai Baba and Maitreya work together all the time. He said that whenever he was asked this question at a lecture he was overshadowed by Sai Baba who gave a blessing to everyone present. This would happen now, he said, and would immediately be followed by a blessing from Maitreya. That way we could experience their relationship for ourselves.

A blessing from Sai Baba

I became incredulous. Looking at the rows of faces, I thought they appeared to be gullible, too accepting of this guru-from-India talk, too ready to believe almost anything with a spiritual message.

I had so enjoyed the lecture about Maitreya's mission in the world that I resented the unexpected intrusion of this unknown being. As Creme raised his right hand, and the presumed Sai Baba began to bless the crowd at the far side of the auditorium, I had nothing but negative thoughts. Maybe the previous night's meditation had been too much for me. This Sai Baba interlude, I thought, just distracted from the important story of Maitreya.

I was probably the only person in the room who did not accept Creme's statement about Sai Baba and his relationship with Maitreya. "Who is this guru in India?" I thought, "What possible connection could this guru have with Maitreya and the reappearance story?"

Creme suddenly stopped and dropped his hand to his side. He was looking around the room as if trying to find someone. People began to be restive. As I looked at him, our eyes met.

A push from the Avatar

He strode to the edge of the stage nearest me and raised his hand. Immediately, a feeling just like the night before hit me. As if it were real and solid, the invisible energy seemed to be pushing me like a strong wind blowing across my body. At first I thought that a sudden summer storm had perhaps invaded the room, or small tornado? My mind searched for logical answers.

Bewildered, I watched Creme's hand making circular motions in my direction. His steady emphasis was drawing the attention of the audience upon me, to my embarrassment. My logical brain could find no explanation for this whole scene.

Every atom in my body seemed disturbed. Finally it occurred to me that if this energy actually came from a being of great power named Sai Baba, then, perhaps through telepathy, I could acknowledge him and let him know I recognized the energy.

So I thought, "Sai Baba, if you are actually doing this to me to make me a believer, I will believe in your powers if you stop your focus on me right now."

Perhaps it was a naïve thought but, by design or pure coincidence, the focus on me and the energy suddenly stopped. Instantly, Creme returned to the middle of the stage to continue Sai Baba's blessing to the audience.

I was overwhelmed by all this new awareness of energy. How was this all possible? Why was it taking place tonight? Why was I experiencing it? Confused, I nevertheless realized that these great beings were real and present in the world, even though I could not see them. Now I was going to have to learn about the life and mission of Sai Baba, whose existence I could not deny.

Some years later I was to encounter Sai Baba in an even more dramatic way.

As I drove home that evening, I thought I had probably had all the spiritual adventures I could handle for one weekend. Little did I know that the following night at the public meditation I would have yet another such experience.

Day three: public Transmission Meditation

Sunday evening's event, to which the public had been invited, was held in a hotel ballroom in downtown Baltimore. Almost 150 people had gathered, which was more than I anticipated. Pleased at their interest in this new meditation, I tried to meet as many as possible before the session began.

Benjamin Creme asked the women to be seated on one side of the room and the men on the other. This made things easier for the Masters during the transmission, he explained, because of the polarity of energy between men and women.

I check the lobby for late arrivals

When almost everyone was seated, I thought it would be a good gesture on my part to check the lobby for late-arriving people who might be lost. Even as I went out, this idea seemed to be just a logical-brain excuse for something else. I knew I should not be the person to be looking for late-arrivals since I knew very little about the group or the meditation. Nevertheless, I followed my instincts and headed for the hotel lobby.

The lobby was deserted and there wasn't much street traffic in front. Even the hotel staff and desk clerks were absent. As I turned back toward the ballroom, a young man entered the hotel. Perhaps he was going to join the meditation, I thought, but more likely not, because he did not fill my expectation of how someone should be dressed for the occasion.

His billowing white shirt, black bicycle shorts and backpack were out of place at a Sunday evening's meditation in a staid hotel in Baltimore in 1982. He must be a bicycle messenger or, more likely, a hotel guest returning from a ride, I thought. An unusually tall man, with wavy hair that came down below the shoulders, he had the olive complexion and dark eyes of someone from northern India. When he spoke to me, however, he sounded like a well-educated American. Except for the black shorts, he matched the image I had formed in my mind of what Maitreya looked like!

After a brief response, I found I had little else to say to him. He appeared to want to start a conversation, but I was in a hurry to use the restroom and return to the meditation. Following me into the restroom, he again smiled and said hello, and seemed even more eager to talk. But I was intent on getting back to the meditation.

I hasten to join the meditation

As I entered the darkened ballroom, they were about to begin. Creme was advising the group to relax while focussing the attention high. He said that in order to facilitate the group overshadowing by Maitreya, we were to hold hands. When the overshadowing was beginning Creme would say the words: "The Christ is near"— not physically near, he emphasized, but energetically. I closed the door and turned to locate a seat.

"What is happening here?" asked the same young man, who mysteriously appeared behind me.

I whispered something about Transmission Meditation and how it would help Maitreya emerge.

He said, "Is it open to the public?"

I replied that it was. Doubting the young man would really want to do this, I did not encourage him. He persisted and asked me if he could join the group. Politely, but a bit coldly, I told him that he was welcome and suggested he sit in the vacant seat next to the last man in the row—but quickly, as it was already starting. As I frantically looked for an empty seat somewhere in the front closer to Mr. Creme, the young man followed me.

There was no doubt now that he was pursuing me and I didn't understand why. The impression that he had not intended to participate in the meditation, but wanted to talk to me, grew stronger. Uncomfortable, I tried to find any seat where he could not sit next to me and ask me more questions.

I had my own questions that needed answers. How could this man look so much like the Maitreya I envisioned? Why were there such contradictions in his appearance and speech? Why couldn't I evade him? The thought came to me that he was indeed Maitreya—but in bicycle shorts?! It was ludicrous.

I found a single chair in the front row in the men's section and sat down. The mysterious young man stood at the end of the room looking at me and then began heading down the middle aisle directly toward me. To my relief all the chairs around me were occupied. Immediately, however, the man sitting next to me jumped up and said he preferred to sit with friends. The thought came to mind that perhaps this was Maitreya and he had sent a mental message to the man beside me to suddenly move. My pursuer quickly came and sat next to me, as if it were ordained. Today it is very obvious. At the time it was very disturbing to think that this man intended to sit next to me and nothing was going to interfere with his plans.

The meditation begins

"Place the attention at the top of the head," said Creme. "Be relaxed. Now take the hand of your neighbor."

Thus, I took the hand of the young man, now thought to be Maitreya, and all was quiet.

"The Christ is near," entoned Creme.

I could hardly believe the reality of that statement. The overshadowing commenced. As before, Creme announced the arrival of different energy waves or rays.

A few minutes later the young man leaned against my shoulder and whispered in my ear, "How long are you going to meditate?" I thought it would be best to say nothing.

Once more he leaned against me and whispered rather loudly, "How long is this going to last?"

My first thought was that this man was not interested in meditation. But Maitreya? I whispered back into his ear that it was going to last for many hours. I reverted to thinking that if he were indeed an uninterested party, he would soon depart. But, he did not leave.

A few minutes later he again leaned over against me and said, "I am a very busy person. I cannot stay much longer. Will you help me?"

Now I was very confused. Was he Maitreya or was he not? If not, what sort of help was he looking for, money? If he were simply a beggar, he was an extremely neat and clean person and also very sophisticated.

He leaned over again and repeated that he had to depart soon and needed help.

At this point, I realized this problem could not be solved during meditation. I asked him if he wanted to talk to me further in the hotel lobby. He said yes and we left the ballroom. He was obviously waiting for me to initiate the conversation. I now realize that he did not wish to intrude upon my freewill.

We move our conversation to the lobby

It was in the lobby that I received an experience of him, as Maitreya—an experience that can only be fully understood by the person who has it.

As we entered the still empty lobby, my confusion was complete. This young man acted and looked like no beggar I had ever encountered. Yet it seemed preposterous to think he was Maitreya.

At first he said nothing, so I tried to tell him that this was not a religious group that could offer him help, I was struck by his direct gaze and obvious amusement. Explaining that we were only a group of strangers who had come together to meditate because we believed Maitreya, the Christ, had reappeared in the world, I saw him become increasingly amused, but he said not a word.

The strangeness of the entire situation eventually caused me to stop talking, and for some moments we simply looked at each other. His gaze, so magnetic and full of joy, deeply penetrated my consciousness. It was the beginning of a deep inner awareness that I was speaking with an extraordinary being.

I wondered what he could possibly want from me. So I put the question directly to him, "Why would you need help from me?"

Hearing my question, his expression became very serious. He looked into my eyes and said, "I have many people in the world to care for. I need your help."

The statement made absolutely no sense to me on a practical level, but it went straight to my heart. I was overwhelmed. For some time—I do not know how long—I could not move or think; I simply looked into his eyes in wonderment. The experience of Maitreya had taken place.

Finally, he smiled at me and said, "Thank you very much", and walked out of the hotel into the night.

Unforgettable memory

This experience of Maitreya has never left my mind; it is as vivid today as when the contact took place in 1982. Others who have seen him also describe their experience as something they will never forget. That weekend of Benjamin Creme's visit to the Washington/Baltimore area was truly my initiation into the story of the reappearance of the Christ.

Looking back, I am thankful that Maitreya and the Masters provided me with these dramatic opportunities to accept the reality of their existence. I was left with little choice but to dismiss any lingering doubts I had about the Masters entering our everyday world. Within months, I was to have an even more profound experience.

Further confirmation

Years later one of Maitreya's disciples, a Master of Wisdom, confirmed through Benjamin Creme that this young man in bicycle shorts was indeed Maitreya. Then, in 1988 it was re-confirmed when I saw the first photograph of Maitreya. It was on a CNN broadcast about the appearance of a man in Nairobi, Kenya who people believed to be Christ. In the photo he was dressed in white robes and had a dark beard. Although the man I met in Baltimore was clean shaven, it was clearly the same face.

At that event in Kenya, an open-air healing service, Maitreya appeared out of thin air before a crowd of 6,000 people and then departed in the same manner, simply disappearing before people's eyes. Fortunately, a Kenyan journalist was there with his photographer, and the resulting story was carried by the press internationally. The photos were later passed around the world, and many people recognized the man as someone with whom they too had a profound encounter.

In recent years many people, perhaps thousands, have seen

Maitreya in the course of their daily lives. In contacts with people involved with Transmission Meditation work, he often asks for their help, as he did with me that night in Baltimore. Maitreya always appears in a manner that initially does not call attention to his status as the Christ, but rather presents himself as a regular member of humanity. It is only *after* the experience that people realize this seemingly ordinary man was indeed extraordinary in every way.

Chapter 6

ᔡ Another meeting with Maitreya ᔥ

"The Master is within you.
If you follow the disciplines of life the Teacher teaches you,
the Master reveals himself within you.
Do not be attached to the human form.
The living truth is a matter of experience."
—Maitreya

In 1983, within months of first hearing about Maitreya and the Masters of Wisdom, I was attending a gathering at the home of friends in Washington, DC. There were about 14 people present. Soon after arriving, while chatting with a woman I knew, I suddenly saw a globe of golden light floating around the room. It first appeared at eye level behind her head, then moved steadily to the left.

Half in shock, but deeply fascinated, I watched as the golden globe floated to the corner of the living room and then began following the walls as if it were on some invisible track. It passed around the heads of a group of people who were standing near the corner of the room. I quickly looked back at my friend, but she was talking to me as if nothing had happened. It was obvious she did not see what I was seeing.

In another few seconds the globe had made one complete revolution and was now back behind her head beginning its second trip. This time there were *two* golden globes, attached and moving silently counter-clockwise around the room.

I restrained my urge to be the first to scream, "What are those globes doing here?"

I thought if I looked in the direction of the globes, my friend would notice the strange phenomenon too, and perhaps she'd say something about them. This did not happen. Instead she kept talking, and I watched as now *three* globes floated around the room. They were the size of volleyballs, linked like a chain of pearls, drifting along at a steady speed.

I could not imagine I was the only person seeing them. I could no longer contain my enthusiasm and was ready to shout, "Why isn't anyone saying anything about the globes of light floating around this room?"

When I tried to speak I was unable to utter a single word. I opened my mouth several times, but not a sound would come forth. Thinking that I was choking, people began to slap me on the back. I motioned that my breathing was fine, but I still couldn't make any kind of sound.

In a final attempt to speak, I lost feeling in my legs and suddenly dropped to my knees on the floor. At that moment I very clearly heard a voice in my head saying, "Do not tell anyone in the room what you see."

It suddenly dawned on me that my dense physical world had come in contact with the spiritual world and the two had meshed.

I looked up, and now a whole chain of linked golden globes filled the entire room, continuing their mysterious circular path. After my fall people had rushed to my aid, but now I suddenly felt fine and could speak again. I did not, however, violate the command I had been given to say nothing about the globes of light.

I was offered a chair near the window in the living room and assured everyone I would be fine in a few moments. What I didn't tell them was that I was watching globes of light multiply, row upon row, with each row moving in the opposite direction.

I closed my eyes for a few moments, thinking that if I did so the globes might disappear and all would be right with the world again. Instead, I discovered that, with my eyes closed, I had an even clearer vision of them. The globes had begun to move so fast that there now appeared to be one vast blur of golden light filling the entire room.

Then the walls began to move into a tighter orb around me. I could no longer see anything beyond the tightening circle but could still hear people speaking in the room.

The vision existed with my eyes open or closed, and nothing would change the situation, so I prepared to face the unknown. I noticed that when fear welled up inside me, the wall of light would stop its movement toward me or even retreat. Once I accepted this circle, it rapidly enclosed me in a tunnel of light.

As solid and filled with life as the light tunnel appeared at the time, I believed it was simply a harmless illusion created for some unknown purpose that I would never fathom. Almost immediately, as I relaxed and resigned myself to the experience, it became even more real.

I looked up into the tunnel of light and saw above me a long silver rod with three prongs coming down. Moments later, the prongs settled at three points around my head and began a process of extracting my consciousness from my physical body. I knew I was about to have what people now call an 'out of body experience'.

The scene changes

When I opened my eyes again, I found myself in a different room. I was lying face down on a dark gray carpeted floor, and next to my head was a hole large enough for a human body to pass through easily. As I looked down the hole, I saw the tunnel of light and, far below, my friends sitting very quietly as if sound asleep.

Suddenly, the hole closed. The portal through which I must have just passed was gone and no trace of it existed. This, I decided, must be some technology not currently available to humanity. I was now in another dimension.

The room was dimly lit and circular, approximately 30 feet across, with a domed ceiling. Built-in seating encircled the perimeter wall except where the portal had been. I picked myself up from the floor and continued to look around.

Along the far wall a pale greenish light illuminated a desk-like affair, while strong white light came from the opposite side of the room from behind a barrier that did not reach to the domed ceiling. I had little time to focus on anything for long because a human-like figure, seemingly neither male nor female, stepped forward from behind this barrier but said nothing. We looked at each other for some time before I realized this 'being' was trying to send me a telepathic message and I was slow on the uptake.

I accept an invitation to meet with Maitreya

This figure, which appeared in the dense, brilliant light as a mist-like form, informed me he had been sent as a guide to transport me to a meeting with the Masters. It was made very clear that I had a choice to go with him or to remain with my friends 'below'.

If I declined their invitation, I was informed that I would be returned to the living room and would have no memory of what had just transpired. Since I did not wish to forget such an experience after coming this far, I agreed to go.

I do not know how the 'travel' was accomplished, since I was in a non-thinking state. I awoke again to find myself being carried through a doorway by two men who gently supported me under the arms. Immediately I was informed that I could now walk on my own. We passed through a portal into a huge room, all the while the two men held me by each arm. As we walked toward a circle of other humans, I had time to notice only that I was with a large number of people dressed like me in short white robes. How or when my clothing had been changed I do not know.

I looked back only once to see my two 'sponsors' standing behind me near the portal where we had entered. They were all wearing various types of long robes. I assumed they were all Masters. One of them appeared very friendly as he motioned with his left hand for me to step forward into the front circle. I was relieved to have at least one 'friend' watching over me as this ceremony proceeded.

Suddenly there was a flash of intense light in the center of our circle. Within moments more light flooded in from the area to my right, but at some distance. As we turned to look at the greater light, the expanse of this immense room became evident. Gigantic doors at the far end were being pulled open. I judged them to be 20 feet tall, comparing their height with that of the men pulling them open.

Light flooded in and revealed many men in long robes between myself, my circle of visitors and the door. The men formed themselves into rows that left a wide central path for an entering human figure, bathed in white light and wearing white robes. As he walked through the rows of Masters on each side, his robes flowed as if a breeze were lifting them. I knew it must be Maitreya, although he was still too far away to see clearly.

My meeting with Maitreya[1]

The brilliant figure approached me and I asked if he was Maitreya, the one we call the Christ.

The reply was "yes", and without further query from me he said, "From time to time the Masters and I invite members of humanity here whom we believe are prepared to assist us in our task."[2]

He asked, "Do you wish to help us?"

Naturally, I said "yes".

He then asked if I would be willing to answer some questions that would help him to assess how I would be most useful to their work. He informed me that I would not remember the questions he asked or the answers I gave. I had some foolish concern that I would honestly give an incorrect answer, but Maitreya laughed at my thoughts and assured me that was not possible. He made it very clear that he would simply read my mind. It was at this point he politely asked me if I was aware that the conversation was totally telepathic. I told him I was not aware of this fact, and immediately some of the Masters began to laugh. Then I too found it humorous that I could not tell the difference between telepathy and regular speech.

For those who have not yet had, or do not remember having, such an experience it is well to consider what is meant by an out of body experience. I discovered that 'reality' is where the consciousness resides at any given time. Standing there in my 'body of light' seemed as physical as my dense physical body feels to me now. There is a sense of touch, even of pain. In most ways I was still in a body I was familiar with in almost every way. Thinking, seeing and touching appeared to me to be no different than when I was standing on solid ground in a solid body. I was reminded of the Ancient Wisdom which teaches that all humans actually have *two* physical bodies, one dense and one energy.

After the questioning was completed, my sponsors turned me in another direction, and I now experienced a spiritual fire blazing before me. I had the urge to reach out and touch the fire. The flames were like magnets, powerfully attracting my attention. I knew these flames represented the three spiritual fires of the cosmos. And in the Bible God is referred to as an all-consuming flame. Amazingly, I was still able to ask Maitreya questions while this wonderful experience was taking place.

Time did not seem to exist. I thought that years might have passed. I was experiencing the 'eternal now' described by sages throughout history. As we stood there with spiritual energy flowing freely, I told Maitreya that, if people could experience this energy, they would discard all their earthly notions of 'paradise'. He laughed and agreed this was a unique experience and that, indeed, the human mind could not comprehend paradise.

He went on to explain that there are other and even greater experiences of God that are far more powerful. "I know," he said, "because I have experienced them."

Too soon, it seemed, I was positioned in another direction, no longer able to see the flames. I was being prepared to leave behind this glorious experience and return to my friends.

Time for a few more questions

I asked Maitreya to answer a few more questions. The two Masters who were accompanying me said there was no time, my friends could not be kept waiting any longer. Maitreya, however, agreed to my request.

My experience had been so profound that I was not sure what I would be returning to on earth. So I asked Maitreya if my old body was still alive and if I was going back to inhabit it. He laughed and assured me that, yes, it was waiting for me. The Ancient Wisdom Teachings now make more sense to me after this experience because they always refer to our physical bodies as merely a vehicle for the soul. It is consciousness that matters.

I then asked if I had to go back to my life in Washington. To my mind, everything in Maitreya's world appeared far more pleasant and I wanted to remain.

He paused for a moment and then asked me, "What is it that so attaches you to the physical world?"

"Nothing," I protested, for at that moment there *was* nothing I wanted to go back to on earth. He looked at me in a curious way and said he wanted to show me something.

We walked over to what appeared to be a blank wall. He moved his hand in a circular motion and, immediately, a 'window' opened onto the world below. Then Maitreya said, "Look out there and tell me what you see."

The most obvious thing was that we were high above the earth, at night, with the sun rising on the far horizon to my right. Below us was a huge desert. At first I searched for the Red Sea or the Gulf of Persia, thinking I could identify the desert below if I could find a recognizable body of water. However, there was no water in sight, only endless land, mostly in darkness.

However, as the rising sun began to shed its first morning light, a vast ocean appeared and I could see the faint outline of the Japanese islands on the far horizon to my right. From that landmark, I reasoned we must be high above the Gobi Desert.

"Yes, yes," said Maitreya, "but that is not what I am asking you to see. Look again and deeper."

This time he placed his hand on me and instantly I floated off into many channels of consciousness at once, viewing the wonders of man's achievements in high culture in both the East and West simultaneously. I can only explain this state of consciousness by asking you to imagine being placed in the center of a large room where the walls are covered with television sets—hundreds of them—all tuned to different stations and broadcasting in various languages. Instead of being able to take in only one station at a time, imagine being able to easily comprehend what is happening on all the stations *simultaneously*. This is how I believe Maitreya relates to the world, having the ability to see and understand what is happening everywhere from moment to moment.

Maitreya asked if I liked what I was seeing and suggested I could stay as long as I liked, that there was no hurry. He kept repeating, "There is no rush."

Indeed, I was happy to keep looking at these scenes; they were all very pleasant. Then he asked if I would like an entire life to experience these earthly events. I replied that it was all so wonderful I wouldn't mind at all.

"How about *two* lifetimes of this experience?" he offered. "There is no rush."

I suddenly realized what I was saying: I had just told him I was *very much* attached to earthly experiences. Maitreya knew he had taught me something about my attachments and that I understood the experience he had just given me. He immediately pulled me back inside the 'portal of experience' and the window closed.

I am reminded of my promises

I had nothing more to say but was overwhelmed by his love when he said, "If I could go back and live the rest of your life for you, I would do it. I would do it for you and for the rest of humanity, but I cannot because I am not allowed to." He reminded me again that I had to live my own life.

Just as my sponsors, the two Masters, were leading me away, Maitreya added, "When the time comes, I hope you will keep the promises you made to me this day."

I told him I did not remember making any promises, but he assured me that I had, and that I would be asked to keep them when the time was right.

I return to my friend's gathering

Humbled by this experience, I was ready to go back to life in Washington and my government job. I was returned to my friend's living room in some unknown manner, but with tremendous speed. The impact of the re-entering my physical body was so great that I bounced off the chair. I opened my eyes to find myself lying face-down on the floor. I pulled myself up on my knees and looked around.

The room was dark and quiet, and I realized that everyone in the house was in some kind of sleep. I wanted to leave before any of them awakened, but as soon as I stood up and took a step toward the door, the lights went on and everyone in the room came to life and started talking. No one seemed to be aware that they had lost an hour that night. As I was leaving, one woman remarked about how she had just looked at her watch and it was eight o'clock, but now it was after nine. The others made no comment, and I quickly rushed home to reflect alone upon the events of that evening.

What happened over the next few days I do not know. My first reality check came when the telephone rang. My office was calling to ask why I hadn't been to work in three days. A good question—with no answer.

Chapter 7

ဆာ Hawaiian night school ◌

"My heart embraces all who know me,
who come to me for help.
Thus shall it always be.
My brothers and sisters, my help is yours
to command: you have only to ask."
—Maitreya

As I began to absorb the importance of this contact with Maitreya and the Masters, I realized that I needed to prepare myself to better understand their role in relation to humanity. I took the suggested reading list in Mr. Creme's book and began my study with the works of Alice Bailey, Helena Blavatsky, Krishnamurti and a few others. I continued with Transmission Meditation on a weekly basis and found others who had also experienced the Masters. I soon realized that my experience was not entirely unique.

After the meeting with Maitreya somewhere above the Gobi Desert, I became accustomed to being awakened at 4:00 a.m., as if I had been startled by something. At times I saw figures of men moving about my bedroom. In the beginning I thought my house was being burglarized. Soon I realized that the Masters often visit us and impart lessons as we sleep, usually arriving at 3:00 a.m. and leaving an hour later.

The 1989 experience

I discovered that I tended to awaken at the moment of a Master's departure. But some years later in 1989 the pattern changed. It was early March and I was on official travel for the U.S.

Government. I had completed a month-long inspection tour of several American embassies in East Asia and the Pacific region. Returning to Washington from Australia, I decided to stop over for one night in Hawaii before continuing my flight.

I arrived in Honolulu in the early afternoon and napped for several hours, then ate at a restaurant along Waikiki Beach. Feeling well rested and well fed, I walked for hours on the beach, enjoying the beautiful Hawaiian evening. I ended my walk with a tour of the old Royal Hawaiian Hotel, which was curiously empty of guests and staff. So I decided to return to my own hotel and arrived there just before 3 a.m.

The first thing I did was open the sliding glass doors to the balcony and let in the balmy night breeze. I felt fortunate to have a room on the 12th floor with an excellent view, especially since I was only paying the government rate. Below me was the ocean and straight ahead, across the green tropical park, was the famous Diamond Head mountain. The rising full moon lit up the ocean and brilliantly outlined Diamond Head against the night sky. There was nothing in this peaceful Hawaiian setting to forewarn me that I was about to have a startling encounter.

I had just started to appreciate the beautiful view, when suddenly I felt as if the room were moving. Instinctively, I grabbed for something to steady myself. My right hand reached out toward the TV set and came down hard on the digital clock, now reading 3:00 a.m. exactly. It flashed through my mind that 3:00 a.m. is the hour when the Masters of Wisdom routinely contact people, but I dismissed that possibility because I thought those contacts usually take place when a person is sleeping. Yet here I was, wide-awake.

My instructor arrives

So, when I looked away from the clock, I was more than a little surprised to find a young man in a short white tunic standing on my balcony. His hair was golden and sparkled in the moonlight. It also stood in long peaks on his head and flowed down to his shoulders. He truly looked like an angel, though I was soon to discover his true identity.

His first words to me were, "I am here to give you your lesson for the day."

I was in shock. I sank onto the bed wondering how this could be happening. I wiggled my toes and touched my body to assure myself I was not dreaming. Surely this was a creation of my mind; but try as I might to dispel the illusion, nothing could make the scene change.

Everything *appeared* to be normal, except that somehow there was a golden-haired boy/man now sitting cross-legged on my balcony. I was far too confused to focus on what he was saying.

My distracted state apparently did not please him, as he suddenly stood up and said, "If you are only going to play mind games and not listen to me, I have better things to do." With that he departed from the balcony by simply passing through the steel railing, walking out upon thin air, and disappearing.

Immediately I heard a voice coming from behind me near the door, "I have sent my disciple to teach you. This lesson is important."

I was being reprimanded for not paying attention to the young Master by another figure clad in darker robes. This apparently older Master, who had also appeared 'out of the blue', continued to express his displeasure and I thought to myself, "Wow! Is he stern."

He must have read my thoughts because, just before vanishing, he gave me a quick smile and a wink.

Now I recognized him! There was no doubt in my mind: he was the one who had held my arm during my meeting with Maitreya some years before. Even his clothing was the same.

Instantly the young man with the golden hair returned and started in on 'the lesson for the day': Self-realization. At first I asked for a different topic, but was promptly told it was the lesson I needed more than anything else. This is the essence of what he conveyed to me in the ensuing hour.

The 'Self' is what might be called the 'Divine Spark' that resides within every human being. To experience and act from that high place is the goal of our incarnational experience. To understand this, we must also know what the Self is not. It is not our mind, spirit or body. In a line from a prayer taught by Maitreya it says, "Mind, spirit and body are my temples, for the Self to realize in them my supreme Being and Becoming."

Being refers to our true Self, the God within, which is eternal. Becoming refers to a process in time and space, our soul's evolution during earthly life. Mind, spirit and body have a beginning and an end. Therefore, freedom of our true Self from mind, spirit and body becomes salvation.

Self-realization is not a philosophy or method; it is simply knowing who we are. Yet it is difficult to achieve because we are conditioned from birth to think of ourselves only in terms of mind, spirit and body. The best way to recognize this conditioning is to observe ourselves in relationships with others. The conflicts that arise with others in daily life are very revealing. We all like to think our views of the world are best or the most correct, even when they are in direct conflict with what is actually happening.

Observe your actions, thoughts and emotions. Give attention to the fact of what *is*, not what *should be*. Such correct observation of life is awareness, which allows us to see the conditioned state in which we perpetually live. Out of this awareness a door will open—it is magical—and the Self will be discovered, if only for a moment.

The greatest obstacle to Self-realization is that we do not want *true* freedom. We love our ideologies, relationships, traditions and leadership from others. We do not want to give these things away. We prefer to have others tell us what is right or wrong. Did we but know it, this is imprisonment. If we choose freedom, then we must give up all these attachments to the familiar trappings of society. This means setting aside the usual mental processes for a period of time and opening ourselves to the true Self.

Detachment from our conditioning requires discipline and is an art that Maitreya will teach us in the coming time. With detachment *anything can be accomplished*. It is the only way to experience the Spiritual Kingdom. Anything done with detachment is divine, as it does not cling to mind, spirit or body.

All in good time

The lesson ended at exactly 4:00 a.m. I enjoyed the teaching and the conversation immensely and hoped that the young Master would stay longer, but he would not.

Before he left, I asked if I would be able to remember any of the lesson the following day. He assured me that I would, perhaps not everything at once, but all in good time.

Chapter 8

∽ Waters of life ∾

"My return among you is a sign
that men are ready to receive new life.
That New Life for men do I bring in abundance.
On all the planes this Life will flow,
reaching the hearts and souls and bodies of men,
bringing them nearer to the Source of Life Itself.
My task will be to channel those
Waters of Life through you."
—Maitreya

Already humanity is being offered special blessings from Maitreya as the 'Aquarian Christ', a name often given to him because he chooses to manifest himself among humanity at the beginning of the age of Aquarius, and promises to remain with us until the end of that age.

One of the most obvious gifts he offers humanity at this time is the springs of healing water being discovered in various parts of the world. The constellation Aquarius is known, astronomically, as the 'Water Bearer', and for thousands of years, in both East and West, the recognized symbol for Aquarius has been water, or a man carrying a pitcher of water. So, to me, it is no coincidence that these springs of water are appearing now, offering healing and spiritual tonic for all people.

I first heard about this particular phenomenon from my parents who were living in southern Texas at the time. Neighbors told them how their own mother had been cured of cancer after drinking the 'blessed' water from a small Mexican village.

Tlacote, Mexico—1991

Jesus Chahin is a prosperous rancher in Tlacote, a small town about a two-hour drive north of Mexico City. In the spring of 1991, Mr. Chahin noticed that his injured dog was recovering very rapidly after drinking the water surfacing from an underground spring on his land. After testing the water on thousands of his animals and on ranch workers who requested it, Mr. Chahin was amazed with the results and opened his property to the public.

It is estimated that several million people have actually visited the ranch to collect water. They come from as far away as Russia and have included well-known personalities from Mexico and abroad. The 'miracle water' has also found its way into the hands of millions more people who use it for healing purposes. In the early years it was quite an ordeal to obtain the water for oneself. Long, unsheltered lines of people sometimes stretched for miles under the hot Mexican sun. Today the process is much more efficient and people no longer have such a long wait. The water is collected and stored in huge stainless steel tanks, from which it is quickly dispensed by ranch workers.

The Chahin family prepares a registration file on every visitor, and then their medical records are checked by Mrs. Chahin, the resident doctor, who suggests the appropriate 'dosage' of water. It can be taken orally, used in the form of eye drops, or applied directly to the skin. No one is charged for these services, and the water is free to all. The office at the Chahin ranch is filled with rows of shelves containing patient files. Many have claimed miraculous healings from illnesses as diverse as cancer, AIDS, diabetes, epilepsy, and arthritis.

In a four-part series on Tlacote broadcast August 5, 1993, on the CBS television program, "Up-to-the-Minute", a San Antonio woman, Hilda Menchaca, said she suffered from rheumatoid arthritis and walked only with the assistance of a walker during her first visit to Tlacote. During her second visit, she needed only a cane. After her third trip, Menchaca walked without any assistance at all. Another resident reported an improvement in her glaucoma and lower blood pressure, while a third said that a proposed organ transplant did not have to take place because of the Tlacote water.

The CBS reporter on "Up-to-the-Minute", Patti Elizondo from KENS-TV in San Antonio, said her own case of viral conjunctivitis was healed in a week, after an ophthalmologist predicted a three-week recovery period. The doctor could not explain the cure, and said the recovery was a 'miracle'.

On October 19, 1992, *The Dallas Morning News* reported on a woman whose brother's diabetes improved, and granddaughter's epilepsy became better after drinking Tlacote water. The article quoted another woman who had been fighting severe arthritis for 30 years. She can now walk with the help of a walker. Her doctors, she said, "couldn't believe it".

Mr. Chahin tells the story of one visitor who drank the water and was healed. The man took many photos of the ranch and the site of the well. On returning home, he had one frame left on his film. Anxious to develop it, he finished the roll by taking a photograph of his new television set, which was not turned on at the time. When the film was developed, the last exposure showed yet another miracle: the distinct image of Christ with a crown of thorns on his head. It was as if he were appearing on television. A copy of that photo, which I believe to be a kind of 'calling card' from Maitreya, now hangs on the wall of Mr.Chahin's office.

Nadana, India—1992

Tlacote is not unique. Another healing water source was discovered in India near New Delhi in 1992. A well that had long been dry filled up with water with miraculous healing power, according to a report in the Japanese media. As many as 20,000 people a day have taken water from this healing source.

Nordenau, Germany—1992

In January of the same year, a spring of pure water was discovered in a cave in a disused slate mine in Nordenau, Germany, 100 kilometers east of Dusseldorf. The land belongs to Theo Tommes, whose Hotel Tommes lies near the quarry. The grotto was investigated by experts who found that it was highly charged with energy. Hundreds of people visit the grotto each day, with buses bringing the old, sick and crippled to 'Germany's Lourdes'. The German newspaper *Bild* reported that Dr. Hans Steinbruck, a general practitioner from Frankfurt, had conducted a study of visitors to the Nordenau healing water spring. Over a four-month period he observed 42 volunteers, most of whom had chronic diseases including rheumatism, muscular atrophy, migraine headaches, allergies and psychiatric illnesses. The study was carried out on a strict medical basis as a clinical trial. Dr. Steinbruck found that 30 percent of the patients were completely cured, while 28 percent showed substantial signs of recovery.

China—1994

The German newspaper *Die Suddeutsche Zeitung* reported in 1994 on a Chinese couple, Zhou Lianghua and his wife Li Guirong, who think they have discovered a fountain of youth. Both are over 80 but claim to feel 10 years younger since drinking the water from their courtyard fountain. Li says that her formerly gray hair has regained its black color, and Zhou, who was almost bald, now has a thick head of hair. They report they can also hike in the mountains without losing their breath.

Russia—1996

In early 1996 a water source that is said to cure alcoholism was discovered in a northern Russian village, according to *Itar-Tass* news agency. "Despairing wives are leading husbands who are on drinking binges to the mystical source," *Tass* said. "The rumor goes that some people have even managed to turn themselves into complete teetotalers." The water source appeared at the site of an unused well that had not been blocked properly.

More to come

According to Benjamin Creme, these waters have been 'magnetized' (and thus given healing properties) by Maitreya, the World Teacher, prior to his appearance to a group in the vicinity. He wishes people to make a connection between the healings that the water brings about and his subsequent appearance. Eventually Maitreya will create 777 such healing water sources, and the use of this 'miracle water' will significantly improve human health worldwide.

Maitreya, the Water Bearer

I had my own 'water experience' at one of Benjamin Creme's lectures in New York City. That afternoon, as I entered the Hotel Pennsylvania ballroom, my eyes locked onto those of an extraordinary woman who stood some distance away inside this huge room. Her head was covered in 'tubes' of golden hair. As I ambled across the room, her eyes never left mine. What wisdom she exuded through them! I wondered how any person could be so magnetic, and I walked as slowly as possible to savor every moment of her gaze.

What struck me was that none of the people passing by, or standing within inches of her, took any notice. She was carrying a huge cloth bag with a wide shoulder strap. The designs and colors reminded me of handicrafts I had often seen in Central America and Mexico. The bag was bulging with small bottles of water.

How strange, I thought. As I stood directly in front of her, I looked down into the bag of water bottles. We exchanged only a few words since Mr. Creme was already speaking and I did not wish to disturb others in the room.

I had intended to return to this woman later and inquire about the water, but she disappeared before I could return. I later discovered that, with the exception of one or two others, no one saw this extraordinary lady. One man claimed to see a woman standing in that location with water bottles, but described her appearance and clothing quite differently from what I had experienced.

Only later did I stop to consider that no ordinary person could have lifted so much water with so little effort. I also speculated that the bottles of water were from the healing well in Tlacote, Mexico. So here was Maitreya, appearing to me as a woman, carrying bottles of water in a huge cloth bag probably made in Mexico. It was as if he were shouting, "Here I am, offering the world the gift of my healing water. Don't you recognize me?"

The Teacher for the age

With his disciples 2,000 years ago, the Christ enacted a dramatic symbolic episode which pointed to his future work in the age of Aquarius. Before the Last Supper he instructed the disciples to go into the city, where they would meet a man carrying a pitcher of water. They were to follow him to an upper room and there prepare for the communion meal. The taking together of bread and wine symbolized the Principle of Sharing, the keynote of the coming age, and the implementation of right human relations on a worldwide scale.

As we move into this new age of Aquarius, our activities are more and more governed and conditioned by the energy of Synthesis. The present turmoil and upheavals are partly due to the 'conflict' between the old separative and individualistic energies which are gradually withdrawing and the new synthesizing energies which are now making their impact felt. The current situation of extreme polarization in the world is largely caused by the crumbling of the old order. However, with Maitreya and the Masters living and working openly among us, the effects of this cosmic shift can, if we so choose, be mitigated.

In *Maitreya's Mission*, Volume I, Benjamin Creme reveals something of what we may expect in the not-too-distant future:

"The Christ comes today to serve the world, to act as the Agent of God, the Avatar, the World Teacher for this age. He says, 'I am the Water Carrier.' He brings the Waters of Life, the new livingness that He releases on all planes. He brings a new potency to our life, on the physical, the emotional and on the mental and spiritual planes. We are entering into an entirely new kind of livingness such as only the very advanced initiates can possibly be aware of up until now. This will become the reality for the vast majority of people. The race as a whole will make this tremendous step forward into becoming the world disciple."

Chapter 9

❧ Sai Baba visits again ❧

"I have come to light the lamp of Love in your hearts,
to see that it shines day by day with added luster.
I have not come on behalf of any exclusive religion.
I have not come on any mission of publicity
for any sect or creed or cause;
nor have I come to collect followers for any doctrine.
I have no plan to attract disciples or devotees
into my fold or any fold.
I have come to tell you of this unitary faith,
this spiritual principle,
this path of Love, this virtue of Love,
this duty of Love."
—Sathya Sai Baba

In October of 1995 I invited John, a childhood friend, to visit for several days. John needed a break from caring for his dying mother in Los Angeles. I had suggested that he read *Maitreya's Mission*, Volume II by Benjamin Creme during his visit. He completed the 718-page book the day before he left. On our last evening together, since he seemed open to the ideas in Creme's book, I decided to tell John about Sai Baba, the 'Man of Miracles' in India.

After my first encounter with Sai Baba's blessing in 1982, I had purchased several books about him and enjoyed reading of the remarkable experiences so many people have had in his presence. A large and impressive collection of people from various countries and religions visit Baba in India each year and come away confident that they had met an embodiment of God. Through my own experiences, I have come to believe he is a God-like being who will more fully reveal himself to humanity after Maitreya's Day of Declaration. So I was anxious to share such hopeful information with a friend in need.

Flowers in the house

As I began to talk about Sai Baba, the room filled with the powerful fragrance of flowers. John immediately asked where the scent was coming from. He got up and started rushing around the living room, then the kitchen and bathroom, trying to locate the source of the perfume. I, too, was baffled by the mysterious and powerful aroma. We searched in vain for several minutes and then, suddenly, it stopped. Then, as soon as I began to speak again about Sai Baba, the scent of flowers was back, stronger than before. We fled to another room to escape the overpowering aroma, but to no avail.

Flowers outside

Although the perfume had a wonderful, sweet smell, we started to cough from the vapors and finally retreated to the outdoor balcony. John suggested there might be a problem with the ventilation system of the house, but we remained perplexed. After a short discussion about the mystery, I resumed talking about Sai Baba as we sat outdoors.

The sweet aroma suddenly returned as I spoke Baba's name, and this time John said, "Is that jasmine?" The question reminded me of a story I had heard about Sai Baba leaving the scent of jasmine as his 'calling card', just as the scent of roses is often associated with the apparitions of the Blessed Mother. I told John I thought the perfume had to be coming from Sai Baba.

Flowers wherever I go

John walked toward me and began sniffing the air in my direction. He came closer and closer and finally exclaimed that the jasmine scent was coming from *me*, specifically from the area of my heart. Since it was right under my nose, I was not aware of the scent being stronger in one location than another. Wherever I went, so did the flower fragrance, but when I stopped speaking of Sai Baba, the sweet aroma also stopped.

I explained to John that this must simply be Sai Baba letting us know that he was aware of our conversation about him. Logical as that seemed to me, my friend was visibly shaken. His hands started shaking, and he said he needed to lie down and rest. Clearly he was in a state of anxiety. So I suggested we both retire for the evening, especially since he had to catch a flight to California in the morning.

During the night I heard John moving about in the house. It was not until I woke the next morning that I realized he was gone. He had been just too disturbed to remain in my home after the experience from Sai Baba and had taken a taxi to the airport where he spent the night.

As soon as he returned to Los Angeles, John looked for a book on Sai Baba. He found one in a bookshop but, when he went to pay the cashier, she said the book did not belong to the shop so she couldn't charge him for it.

John took his free book to the hospital and read one chapter each day to his ailing mother, hoping to comfort her as best he could. She was an atheist and very much afraid to die, as she believed there was nothing after death but a total void. Nothing during her life had convinced her of the existence of God or life after death.

Now she appeared to be perfectly content listening to her son read her stories about the Avatar in India. In fact, when John finished reading the last chapter, she told him she could now die happily, since she had a new belief in life after death.

When John arrived home that evening, the phone rang. Someone from the hospital informed him that, just minutes after he left, his mother had passed away. He rushed back and, when he got there, three of the attending nurses, who knew his mother well from her stay, told him that a most unusual event had occurred.

At the moment of her death, as the three nurses watched in awe, a white vapor rose from her body and circled the room. It then departed through the window and vanished. Never had they experienced anything of this sort. I firmly believe that Sai Baba was with John's mother at the moment of her death and that he created the vapor to prove to everyone that there is something beyond physical death.

I also think the attention John and I received from Baba that final evening at my home was to help him deal with the impending death of his mother.

Sai Baba's mission

Sai Baba is considered by many to be an Avatar, one of those representatives of the Godhead who come occasionally to earth to help and enlighten humanity. Benjamin Creme describes him as a 'Spiritual Regent', and affirms that Sai Baba and Maitreya work in close collaboration for the betterment of humanity and the planet.

Sai Baba was born in the remote village of Puttaparti, Andhra Pradesh, India on November 23, 1926 and has only left India once in his lifetime. He makes his home in an ashram in Puttaparti, where tens of thousands of people from around the world come to visit him each year.

Sai Baba is often called the 'Man of Miracles'. He materializes objects, as if from thin air, and is famous for producing vibhuti, an ash-like substance that his devotees eat as a blessing, not unlike

Christians who partake of the body and blood of Christ in the communion wafer and wine. He once created a rainbow at high noon in a hot desert climate for a group of Harvard scientists, demonstrating that he has control over the natural elements. He has also been known to raise a dead man to life.

I have never traveled to India to visit Sai Baba, but I have experienced his presence in other ways on several occasions. My direct spiritual contact with the energy or force of Sai Baba's essence has made me a believer in his superhuman powers and proved that he is indeed a messenger from God.

Chapter 10

ᕙ Clues from around the world ᕗ

"Wherever you may look in the world today
you will find change.
From top to bottom the fabric of the old
and decaying order is rent.
From this can we derive much satisfaction,
for despite the pain involved in this process,
a new and better world emerges.
Therefore, my friends, take comfort from this fact
and look to the future with hope."
–Maitreya

There are many people who are convinced of Maitreya's presence mainly on the basis of the miracles taking place in the world today. Others, including people in positions of leadership around the world, are convinced of his presence based upon their own personal experiences. Over the past several years, I have met a number of individuals in this latter category.

Unlike myself, they may not be aware of the historical writings about the coming of a World Teacher or of the current lectures by Benjamin Creme. Their experiences are mainly through direct contact with Maitreya or one of the Masters of Wisdom. Some are reluctant to speak openly of their involvement with the emergence of Maitreya, as such disclosure would limit their usefulness in current activities vital to the preparations for the new time. Others, who could and probably should speak out, do not do so for fear of public condemnation.

My contacts with such individuals began while I was working in Washington, DC as an official of an independent agency of the

White House. That position gave me a level of credibility and also access to people at important levels of business and government.

While attending diplomatic receptions, private parties with the 'movers and shakers' of the Washington political scene, and through contacts overseas, I eventually discovered others who knew about and were interested in the emergence of Maitreya. I no longer felt alone in my conviction that these extraordinary Teachers are contacting humanity, and not just randomly but with specific intent. Many of those contacted are people in positions of power who can bring about the needed changes in various fields of endeavor to usher us into a new era of global cooperation. Without the help of these influential people, it is doubtful that the plans of the Masters could go forward, or at least with the speed that is called for in today's chaotic world.

The majority of my contacts revealed that the Masters themselves insisted they keep a low profile with the public. I can only conclude that Maitreya does not want anyone in a position of influence or authority to speak for him or attempt to convince the public of his presence. He wants people to experience him directly and to draw their own conclusions.

Maitreya's message and priorities will become perfectly clear to humanity when he speaks on international television. In communications he has given through different individuals, he has emphasized that no group, religious or otherwise, should try to claim him exclusively for themselves. He works with and through all men and women of goodwill who long for a world characterized by sharing, brotherhood, justice and peace.

The following stories about public figures do not, in themselves, prove the existence of Maitreya and the Masters. They are, however, part of a large body of evidence I have accumulated in the past 18 years that some magnificent spiritual force is gently guiding us in the direction of a safer, saner world. My conviction that it is the work of the Spiritual Hierarchy comes from my own direct experience, but I do not ask you to draw the same conclusion or even take my word for it. I merely invite you to consider the possibility.

A meeting of world leaders

In April 1988 a close associate of Maitreya, long established in London's Asian community, began a series of briefings in which he presented excerpts from Maitreya's teachings and forecasts of world events. The information, given to two London-based journalists, was made available to the world's press and also published, as received, in issues of *Share International* magazine.[1]

In that same year he informed the journalists that Maitreya was now contacting large numbers of influential people on a regular basis. Then, in early 1990, he said that a meeting would be held near London to inform diplomats, journalists, members of royal families, political leaders, representatives of the world's religions, scientists, educators and others about the coming global changes and how they could play an important part within their own spheres of influence. The April 1990 issue of *Share International* magazine (published in late March) said this momentous meeting would take place during the last week of April.

I had my doubts that such a high-level, by-invitation-only meeting could take place without word leaking to the press, but it seemed like a perfect opportunity for me to investigate further.

I began to scrutinize the international news for any hint of a global conclave. I really didn't expect to see much, since the schedules of heads of state are contained only in classified documents in an attempt to minimize risks to their personal safety. So, just a day before the meeting was said to be taking place, I was truly surprised to read that King Hussein of Jordan and Yasir

Arafat, leader of the Palestinians, were both in London on 'personal business'. Hussein's wife, Queen Noor, spent that weekend in New York and, when confronted by the press about her husband's trip to London, she insisted it was nothing official and definitely not related to the Palestinian negotiations.

The Ayatollah declares a cease-fire

Another powerful political figure, the Ayatollah Ruholla Khomeini of Iran, was the supreme head of his country when war broke out between Iran and Iraq in 1980. It was a very bloody affair which lasted until the cease-fire in August 1988.

What interested me was that Maitreya's associate had told the two London journalists that Maitreya was making contact with various world leaders. Those in the Islamic world often recognized Maitreya as the Imam Mahdi, the great spiritual being who the Prophet Mohammed said would come in the future to change the world.

A short time later, just months before Khomeini's death in June 1989, several American newspapers reported that the Ayatollah had spoken to the Iranian people on radio and announced a cease-fire in the war with Iraq. Khomeini reportedly said that he did not want to stop the war but was ordered to do so by God Himself; that it was a bitter pill to swallow, but he could not go against the word of God. Coincidence?

President Bush exercises free will

As mentioned earlier, after I read the *The Reappearance of the Christ and the Masters of Wisdom* by Benjamin Creme, I began to attend a weekly meditation organized by people who were also interested in the emergence of Maitreya. The closest group for me to attend on a regular basis was one in Georgetown, a prestigious suburb of the District, at the home of one of President George

Bush's advisors. The man himself was not a member of the group but allowed his housekeeper to host our meetings.

One evening, while Mr. Bush was having dinner with his associate, he jokingly asked our group hostess if she thought he could win the upcoming presidential re-election. "No, Mr. President," she replied, "Lord Maitreya has already stated that you will not have a second term in office."

When she relayed this story to me later, I could not help but wonder if the president was amused at that new advice or if he might have already heard it from others. I do, however, believe that he understood that Maitreya was a spiritual leader. I thought it curious that the president did not protest or question this very frank statement about his re-election.

According to Benjamin Creme, on information received from the Master with whom he works, "...one of [Mr. Bush's] entourage, a diplomat who had attended the April 21/22 [1990] Conference held by Maitreya in London, suggested to President Bush to send an envoy to London... According to my Master, this has been followed up by the sending of a second envoy, reiterating the Americans' desire for a peaceful solution to the Gulf Crisis and asking for Maitreya's advice... Maitreya said he would guarantee that Saddam Hussein would withdraw all his troops from Kuwait without firing another shot if Mr. Bush were to organize a program of aid for the economy of Iraq." [2]

For me, the connection between President Bush and Maitreya seemed to be supported by an August 1990 newspaper article. According to the report, the president had just completed a briefing for the White House press corps on the expected Middle East conflict. As they departed the briefing, some of the journalists headed around to the east side of the White House grounds, where they noticed Mr. Bush strolling in the rose garden. He was looking in the direction of the Washington monument. Suddenly, a formation of fog surrounded its base. As the journalists watched, the fog rose like a doughnut up the monument until it reached the top. There, the fog formed a perfect cross and then dissipated.

The journalist writing the story was sure that President Bush had witnessed this event along with the people in the area of the monument. He speculated that it might be some spiritual sign or omen, coming as it did directly after a briefing on the coming Gulf War, but he offered no other suggestions as to its meaning. I was convinced, however, that it was Maitreya's last attempt to influence President Bush to oppose military action in the Gulf.

Directly, and through symbol, the president was advised by the Masters, then left to make his own decision—for better or worse. Although the war was short in duration, the price was astronomical in terms of innocent lives lost and destruction of the environment. In the end, nothing had really been accomplished, I believe, that could not have been handled by other means, and the antagonist walked away unscathed. President Bush, on the other hand, extremely popular *during* and just after the war failed to be re-elected. Prior to the election, Maitreya had forecast that the Democratic candidate would be the victor,[3] and he was right.

Cause and effect

Scientists have proven that for every action there is an equal and opposite reaction. Students of the Ageless Wisdom would refer to this principle of nature as the Law of Cause and Effect. Although, as humans, we have a measure of free will, our actions always set into motion causes that will, somewhere down the line, produce a corresponding effect. Wise choices and beneficent actions will beget positive results, while poor choices and destructive actions lead inevitably to negative consequences. It is a totally impartial system and one of the principle laws of the universe that we humans are still learning.

Giorgio Bongiovanni speaks out

One person who is not reluctant to tell his story is an Italian man named Giorgio Bongiovanni, who speaks of having visions of the Madonna, which started in April 1989, and of receiving messages from her. He has met with Queen Sophia of Spain, Mikhail Gorbachev and other top officials in Russia and has spoken at the United Nations. His goal is to "sensitize the consciousness of humanity to the great changes about to occur in the world." To provide evidence that something extraordinary is taking place, he experiences the stigmata[4] on his hands daily.

His story reminds me of the Marian apparitions in Medjugorje, since he too speaks with the Madonna and has received knowledge of secrets, especially the recently-revealed third secret of Fatima.

Fatima, a small town in Portugal, made headlines around the world in 1917 when an apparition of the Blessed Mother appeared to a group of three children over a period of five months. An estimated 70,000 people attended the final event and witnessed the 'miracle of the sun'; that is, the sun appeared to dance in the sky, similar to modern-day events in Medjugorje. The apparition is referred to simply as Our Lady of Fatima, since she never identified herself by name.

At that time, three secrets were revealed to one of the visionaries, 10-year-old Lucia de Jesus dos Santos, now a cloistered Carmelite nun. The first was a message of peace (this was during World War I) and a vision of hell, with anguished souls plunged into an ocean of fire. The second secret prophesied that Russia would "spread her errors through the world, causing wars and persecution against the Church". The third secret, locked in a drawer in the Vatican for 60 years and read by each successive pope, but supposedly too horrible to be revealed, was finally made public on June 26, 2000.

Excerpts from Lucia's 1944 letter, carried by the Associated Press, described what some might call an Apocalyptic vision, cloaked in symbol, of "...Bishops, Priests, men and women Religious, and various lay people of different ranks and positions". Instead of putting to rest decades of speculation, the revelation has fueled a new round of church debate over its meaning and relevance for Catholics.

Missing from the published excerpts was mention of the reappearance of Christ, which Giorgio Bongiovanni claims is part of the third secret: "The Virgin Mary told me that he is not expected, but will come back. In other words, he will come back, but no one expects to see him so soon. I do not know the exact date, but I know that *now* is the time. As it was written in the Bible, he will come and probably no one will be aware that he is here... But eventually everybody will realize it."[5] Is part of Sister Lucia's letter still being withheld by the church?

Franklin Roosevelt and the Masters

Another world leader who had contact with the Masters is Franklin Roosevelt. Evidence of his interest in Masters of Wisdom can be found in the records at the Roosevelt Library in Hyde Park, New York. Apparently, FDR sought the advice of the Masters during World War II through Helena Roerich..

Helena Roerich and her husband Nicholas were natives of St. Petersburg, Russia, but lived many years in India and also spent time in Europe and America. Throughout the war, they resided in an area of northern India near Tibet in what is called the Kulu Valley.

Helena was inspired by one of the Masters to write a number of books, which are still in print. They are part of a collection known as the Agni Yoga Series. During her time in India during the war, she corresponded with the White House and advised

President Roosevelt on a number of matters related to the war effort.

The letters they exchanged were published in 1948 by Westbrook Pegler, a columnist with the Hearst newspapers. This public disclosure had negative repercussions on Vice President Henry Wallace's presidential ambitions, as it seemed indisputable that he had penned these letters for Roosevelt. Because they addressed Roerich as "Dear Guru", the letters came to be known as the FDR "guru letters".

Wallace and Roosevelt knew that care had to be taken not to appear too involved in such an unorthodox spiritual venture, and they never admitted to being the authors. Nevertheless, these letters made interesting reading, since they contained advice to the president on matters pertaining to the war and offered encouragement that it would end triumphantly for the 'forces of light' who were in support of the allied nations.

Henry Wallace was, apparently, an ardent supporter of the Roerich's philosophy, and they communicated over a period of years. It was Nicholas Roerich, for example, who suggested to Wallace that the image of the pyramid on the Great Seal of the United States would be appropriate for the design on the one-dollar bill. Wallace passed this idea onto the secretary of the treasury, Henry Morgenthau, and the image of the pyramid has ever since been printed on the dollar bill.

In 1934, when Henry Wallace was secretary of agriculture, he offered Nicholas Roerich a U.S. Government grant to fund an expedition through China and Mongolia to search for drought-resistant plants. Roerich was very interested in this venture and immediately accepted. His account of their journey, *Heart of Asia*, is fascinating, in no small part from Helena's experiences with Masters along the way.

Nicholas Roerich was also known internationally as an artist and philosopher. Many of his spiritually-inspired paintings of the Masters in Europe and America are in museums and collections around the world.

Nicholas directed efforts to gain support for the Roerich Peace Pact, a treaty written in 1928 that preserved and protected cultural institutions and monuments in times of war. The treaty was eventually signed on April 15, 1935 in the White House in the presence of President Roosevelt and delegates from twenty Latin American countries. For his efforts in this matter, Nicholas was nominated for the Nobel Peace Prize.

Not a 'new age' phenomenon

The existence of the Masters of Wisdom is not a fanciful new age notion but very ancient knowledge which has only been committed to writing and made available to the public-at-large in the last 150 years. I refer you to Appendix I for information on the Ageless Wisdom Teachings and the principle purveyors of this information in modern times.

As the 'elder brothers' and guardians of the human race, the Masters stand ever ready to offer assistance as we gradually plod our way back to the Source of all Being. They work through men and women in every strata of society and in every field of endeavor, and have done so for countless thousands of years. Their emergence into full public view and open collaboration with humanity fulfills part of their own destiny as a group and allows us to take a giant evolutionary leap.

Take a good look at those leaders around you and in the wider world who are working to abolish the old miseries, and I suggest you will find members of Maitreya's vanguard.

Chapter 11

❧ Private meetings with the Masters ❧

"Your experience is your blessing.
What you have experienced, you know.
Others can only understand once they have experienced."
—Maitreya

After years of my following the story of the emergence of the Spiritual Hierarchy, word got around that I was interested in and willing to talk openly about it. From time to time I was asked to speak to a small group or was introduced to someone who had contact with the Masters but who wished to remain anonymous. These contacts were exciting for me and led to many new friendships. One speaking engagement proved to be the most revealing—not for what was said, but for what was *not* said.

I am acknowledged with an eloquent silence

This event was special because it was attended by people who are important to the reappearance of the Christ by virtue of their positions, even if they doubt that the Christ is truly here. Several of the guests were European visitors associated with the Roman Catholic church. One particular gentleman can only be identified as a very close friend of the pope.

The guest list also included a businessman close to the U.S. president, a Jesuit priest from Georgetown University, and others whose names would be familiar to many in the U.S. and overseas.

Therefore, I was somewhat apprehensive about facing this important audience—so closely attached to the Catholic church—with my strange story. I had no idea how much information these people already had on the topic, but assumed it was little or none.

After delivering what sounded to me like a prolonged monologue on Maitreya and his mission, I was shocked when the room remained totally silent. Not even the Jesuit priest sitting next to me said anything—no questions, no denials. Perhaps it was the overpowering presence of a close friend of the pope, I thought, or maybe they already knew as much as I did about it. It just didn't seem possible that *no one* would feel compelled to respond.

The only hint of recognition had come during my presentation, when the man with the White House connection smiled broadly and nodded his head in agreement with some of my statements.

Finally, the host asked the friend of the pope for his opinion. He replied that the Vatican was fully aware of all this, but that it was up to the Holy Father to make a statement.

Nothing further was said on the subject that night, but later I was contacted confidentially by several of the guests. They informed me they, too, are aware of the reappearance but are not prepared to say anything in public or even at a private gathering, presumably because of its potential effect on their reputations. I do know, however, that some very important people have met Maitreya and pledged their support for his work but have been specifically asked by *him* not to speak about it yet. Because they are so influential it might violate the free will of those whom they address. I believe it is intended that everyone will come to recognize the World Teacher from their own intuitive response to his words and his love, rather than by someone's proclamation.

Mr. Jones' 3 a.m. help with a project

One person who confided in me after the meeting was a Mr. Jones (obviously not his real name). When I had presented some of Maitreya's goals, his knowing smile and nods told me this was not news to him. Afterwards, he volunteered his own stories of private meetings with spiritual beings and how they are helping him with a project that is of great importance to Maitreya.

'Meetings with spiritual beings' may not sound too unusual in today's world, since there are many people anxious to tell their latest 'encounter' to anyone who will listen, and scores of books, including this one, are now appearing on the topic. Mr. Jones, however, shared his experiences of the Masters with only a few carefully-chosen people.

When I first met Mr. Jones, I remembered a picture I had seen of him only a few weeks earlier on the front page of the newspaper standing next to President Clinton. I knew he was a successful businessman with contacts at high levels of the government. Therefore, he was unwilling to discuss his experiences publicly, since it could compromise his credibility and negatively affect his work with those in leadership positions. Nevertheless, during the course of a five-hour dinner he confided in me his most extraordinary experiences with the Masters, asking only that I never use his name in connection with these stories.

From my own experience, I immediately recognized the truth in what he was telling me. For one thing, his first experience began at three o'clock in the morning when he was asleep. The time was significant, as the hour between three and four a.m. is said to be when the Masters usually make contact with individuals for teachings purposes.

One night an extremely bright light, coming from somewhere beyond his bedroom door, awakened him. Since he knew he was alone in the house, he believed it couldn't be a normal household light. It was so intense it radiated out from under the door of the guest bedroom, down the hall and under Mr. Jones' bedroom door, waking him from a sound sleep. Yet, amazingly, without any fear, he confidently walked toward the light and opened the door. Suddenly, he was face to face with three strangers.

They looked at him but said nothing; *he* was speechless. Eventually, he recovered enough to ask what they were doing in his house. One of the men finally said, "You invited us; what do you want?" Incredulous at the response, he quickly realized that not only was this an exceptional event, but also these were not ordinary men, as brilliant light blazed from their bodies filling the room and beyond.

The apparent spokesman for the group reminded Mr. Jones that he had been praying for help with his project and they were here in response to that call. Ordinarily he would have considered such a comment ludicrous, but he had indeed been praying for help and now, it seemed, his prayers were being answered. Only one of the men spoke, and I have no doubt that this was Maitreya. The other two would have been Masters who often accompany Maitreya when he appears to people.

The three men not only emitted light to demonstrate their 'other worldliness' but also dressed in a manner that was anything but ordinary. Mr. Jones said they wore shining metal suits for battle, what we would think of as medieval armor. Before they left, he asked about the suits. They replied that they were ready to 'do battle' for his cause. Maitreya and the Masters are not without a good sense of humor and often dress in a symbolic manner.

The following day after that early morning experience, Mr. Jones was en route from the White House to the Capitol building when the same three men simply appeared out of thin air as passengers in his car. The spokesman (Maitreya?) was in the front seat.

He made no apologies for their sudden appearance and informed Mr. Jones that he could now expect them at any time of the day or night. This time, the three men wore ordinary business suits, probably being aware that medieval garb on Pennsylvania Avenue in mid-day traffic would attract too much attention.

Although only the man in the front seat spoke, Mr. Jones could see the others in his rearview mirror. The three disappeared as they had arrived, in a flash into thin air, but not before discussing the business they wanted to accomplish with Mr. Jones. From what I know, the Masters do not waste time and energy with visits unless there is a purpose. I suspect there are a few thousand stories of this type in the United States alone.

A personal friend is directed to Mr. Jones

During a reception with over a thousand people present, one of the Masters appeared to a friend of mine in the form of the Blessed Mother Mary. Now a Master of Wisdom, she told him that a very important person, whose work would do much to improve the well-being of humanity worldwide, was in the room. The apparition led him directly to the man, who was none other than Mr. Jones, and said, "Introduce yourself."

Since only he could see the Blessed Mother at this point, my friend was reluctant to talk to a complete stranger about Masters and holy apparitions. Nevertheless, he was able to convey that they were destined to meet and proceeded to surprise Mr. Jones with intimate knowledge of his work and the mysterious meetings with holy men. That was enough to convince Mr. Jones that he had just met another person who was working with the Masters of Wisdom.

This encounter took place *before* I gave my talk to the group of dignitaries and subsequently met Mr. Jones. It was the Blessed Mother, not I, who gave the information to my friend and prompted the introduction.

For the time being, the nature of Mr. Jones' work may not be revealed. What I can say is that, after Maitreya's Day of Declaration, he will be able to reveal his identity, and the entire world will know of his involvement in an important humanitarian project. He is prepared even now to go forward with it, but Maitreya has indicated the time is not yet right. Humanity has to begin to see itself as one family, sharing the resources of the world, before Mr. Jones and others like him can successfully launch their projects.

World leaders gather

I had contacts in many government agencies, departments, and international organizations based in Washington. I became friends with one well-placed man working with a major international agency. Our talks were not about 'religion' but about the much broader topic of 'spirituality'.

I knew he was preparing to attend a major international conference in Europe for heads of state and world economic leaders. In fact, he was to be the keynote speaker. I thought this was an excellent time to introduce him to Maitreya's thinking on international economic policy, as it is presented in Benjamin Creme's book, *Maitreya's Mission,* Vol. II. When I offered him the book, he hastened to explain that, while he found the idea of Christ's return interesting, he was far too busy to take on additional reading material at this time.

I insisted he take my copy with him, not to read now but just to have available in his library for the appropriate moment. I added that, when the time was right, the Masters would manage to bring the book to his attention. Although he again explained how busy he was going to be for the next month or so, he finally accepted the book.

I did not expect to hear from Mr. Brown for at least several months and was pleasantly surprised when he called me only a few weeks later. He said he had just returned from the economic conference in Europe and had a wonderful experience he wanted to tell me about as soon as possible. I invited him to come to my home the following day, already having an inkling about what may have happened.

The Masters 'plant' my book

He told me that, after boarding his flight, he wanted to spend time polishing his keynote speech. As he reached into his briefcase, instead of pulling out his papers, out came the book I had given him a few weeks before.

He had no idea how that book got into his briefcase. Due to the confidential nature of his business, neither his wife nor his secretary were allowed to open the case, yet there was the book in his hand on the flight to Europe.

With his curiosity thus piqued, he decided to have a cocktail and casually page through the book. The brief scanning soon turned into a full reading, as he realized that some of Maitreya's ideas would make interesting material for his speech. So, without delay, he began to rewrite the keynote address that he would deliver on the following day.

At the opening of the conference, Mr. Brown presented these new ideas to high-ranking economic leaders and heads of state, having no sense of how they would be received. To his surprise, many of the delegates were keenly interested and wanted to know more. So, too, did the ruling monarch of the country hosting the conference.

Mr. Brown was invited to come for lunch at the royal palace the next day. When he arrived, he discovered he was not the only guest, and recognized a number of conference delegates from various countries. Europe, Asia and the Middle East all seemed to be represented. So he began to relax, thinking this was just an informal affair to thank the delegates.

Still he thought, "Why this particular mix of people?"

As the luncheon guests were ushered into the presence of H. Royal Highness, Mr. Brown realized he was being seated next to the monarch.

"Why the honor?" he wondered, since he was not a delegate representing a nation state. When asked if he knew why he had been invited, he replied "no". The monarch then inquired about the origin of the unusual ideas in his keynote speech.

Feeling the moment of truth upon him, he decided to be totally honest. He related the story of my offering him the book *Maitreya's Mission,* how it had mysteriously appeared in his briefcase, and how he read it on the plane and was fascinated with the ideas. H. Royal Highness was now smiling and nodding in approval. The monarch then explained that everyone in the room knew Maitreya and was cooperating with his mission, although their identities must be kept secret until Maitreya himself comes forward and speaks openly to the world.

There was one individual, however, who made it clear he had no problem with the public knowing he had met the Christ. His name was Mikhail Gorbachev. Since he was now out of political power in his country, I assume he felt he had nothing to fear or lose from such a disclosure.

I was not surprised to learn this about Mr. Gorbachev, since I had heard much earlier of his involvement with Maitreya from a Pentagon official. I had also heard, from people I place much confidence in, that Mrs. Gorbachev had been to India several times to see the Avatar Sai Baba. I find it interesting that the international press never questioned Mr. Gorbachev more about his spiritual beliefs, since both he and his wife became Christians during his term in office. From the freedom and openness he introduced to the Soviet Union, it appeared obvious to me that he was being influenced by the Christ. Eventually, we will hear more of this story and how the Soviet empire collapsed.

What I appreciate about this story is the sure knowledge that the Masters have already undertaken the task of offering important world leaders a role in the coming global changes and of preparing them for the Day of Declaration. These leaders, who are undoubtedly disciples of the Masters, will be working to promote the goals of the Spiritual Hierarchy.

Moreover, in one way or another, these individuals have managed to discover each other. Mr. Brown did not tell me their names, but I was able to make some educated guesses. I knew from his response (or lack of response) that I was correct about a few of them.

The Masters have always guided humanity

We are told that the Masters have always inspired and guided humanity, albeit mainly from behind the scenes of everyday life. It does not matter whether we call them Masters, spiritual beings, risen saints, angels or devas. *What matters is that they wish to work with humanity for a rapid transformation of our planetary life.* They now offer their guidance *openly*. It is one of the major roles they play in our planetary scheme.

Their influence is often felt most profoundly by the more advanced men and women who are at the forefront in their various fields of endeavor, such as the great artists, scientists and politicians. Some of these leaders, including Mr. Gorbachev, may consciously know they are being guided by the Masters, but most probably do not. A scientist may talk about a sudden breakthrough in his work, as if by some miracle, when in fact it may be the work of a Master projecting a mental image to him, which is finally comprehended.

Today, this long-standing relationship is being brought to light, as Maitreya and the Masters appear more openly in physical form to both world leaders and ordinary citizens. This will accelerate the pace of new discoveries in all fields, as humanity works in knowing cooperation with its great benefactors to solve the problems of the world.

Wayne Peterson (right) taking the oath of the U.S. Information Agency's Foreign Service before R. Ellsworth Miller, Chief of Recruitment. ... He will probably go to Latin America as he speaks both Spanish and Portuguese. ... Mr. Peterson was born in Shawano [WI] and attended the University of Wisconsin in Madison. For the last two years he has served in Sao Paulo, Brazil as a Peace Corps volunteer. He is now one of the U.S. Information Agency's 1,700 foreign service officers stationed in 104 countries to win support for United States policies and to give the world a true picture of the American people. (From the *Shawano Evening Leader,* January 1967)

In 1966, articles about the successful S.O.S. project appeared in *Folha de Sao Paulo*, Brazil's largest daily newspaper, and *Campinas*, a regional paper. The president of S.O.S., Mr. Helio Audi, and Mr. Peterson are shown here visiting one of the homes under construction. The second photo shows the lots where other homes will be built in the future.

On June 11, 1988, Maitreya, the World Teacher, suddenly appeared before a vast crowd in Nairobi, Kenya, gathered to witness the miracle healings of Kenyan spiritual healer Mary Akasta. Moments before, Mary had interrupted the singing to announce that God had just spoken to her and said that a very important guest would be coming to deliver a vital message.

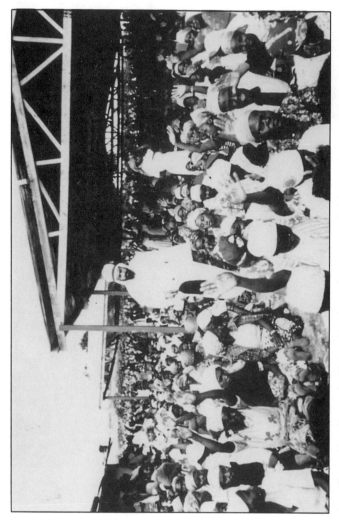

According to Mary Akatsa, the Christ said to her. "I have put my cloth here at the end of the path, and whoever comes to this place—perhaps with sickness or demons or other problems—should run along that path. Then, when he comes back and looks at you, Mami [Mary], all his problems, all sins ... will be healed ..."

Sai Baba of Puttaparti, India is believed by many to be an Avatar, or divine incarnation. "The Avatar comes to reveal man to himself, to restore him his birthright of Atmic bliss. He does not come to found a new creed, to breed a new faction, to instill a new God. ... The Avatar comes as man in order to demonstrate that man is divine, and to be within reach of man." –Sathya Sai Baba

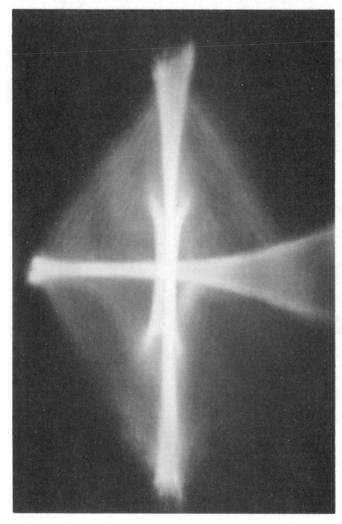

Glowing crosses of light mysteriously began appearing in the windows of homes in the Los Angeles area in May of 1988. Since then, they have been discovered in other U.S. cities and across the globe. In 1995 the most spectacular manifestations appeared in the tiny Copper Ridge Baptist Church outside Knoxville, Tennessee.

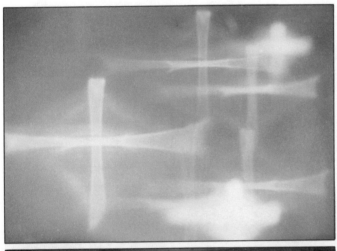

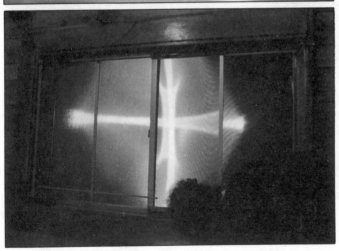

Many say the crosses of light transmit a tremendous healing energy that has cured thousands and transformed the lives of all who come to see them. In the right-hand photo, multiple crosses can be seen due to the presence of numerous light sources behind the glass.

During three weeks over Christmas, 1996, some 450,000 people came to view the wall of a black-glass building in South Florida where a two-story-high image of the Virgin Mary had appeared. The rainbow-colored image is about 50' wide and 35' tall. Said one visitor, "It is awesome. I don't know which I find more compelling—the vision of Mary or the transforming effect on the masses." The image remains to this day.

In December 1992 members of the Vietnamese Christian Community Centre in Pooraka (Adelaide), South Australia noticed what looked like blood streaming down the cheeks of this 12" high statue of the Madonna. When the statue 'weeps', the air fills with the perfume of roses. A sister statue of the Virgin manifested a crystalline 'teardrop' in each eye. Father Augustin Nguyen Duc Thu, who brought the statues to Australia from Fatima, believes the Madonna weeps for the state of the world and is calling Christians back to the true teaching of Jesus. (Courtesy of Hoang Van Hao)

Increasingly, the Masters make their presence known in clever ways, such as impressing an image on a single frame of film. When the roll is developed, something quite different from the original subject appears. In these photos, the image of the Virgin Mary is unmistakable. The right-hand photo was taken at Medjugorje, the left-hand photo somewhere in the American Southwest.

112

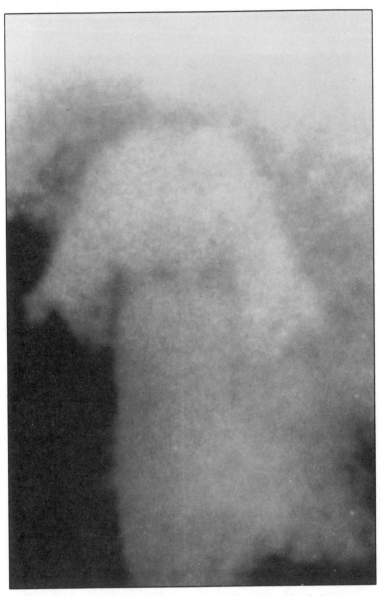

This Christ-like figure is reported to have appeared in hundreds of photos, many taken from the windows of airplanes. At the time the photo is taken, the image is not visible.

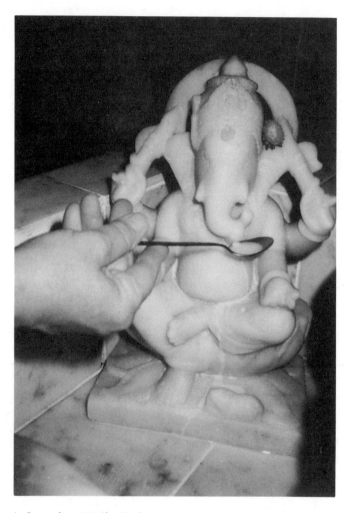

In September 1995 the Hindu community was stunned, as sacred statues began to 'drink' milk offerings. The phenomenon lasted for five days and drew the faithful and skeptics alike into temples around the globe. Ancient Vedic texts state that statues drinking milk will be one of the signs that "a Great Soul has descended".

In various parts of the Islamic world, where statues and images are forbidden, the name of Allah has been appearing in most unusual places. The seeds of this freshly-sliced aubergine (eggplant) form the Arabic script for "Ya-Allah", meaning Allah exists. Similar messages have appeared on or in other fruits and vegetables, eggs, beans, and on the belly fur of lambs and goats. (Photo: News Team International)

The odds of finding a white buffalo are about one in six million. Yet, since 1994, four such calves have been born in the U.S., fulfilling Native American prophecies about the White Buffalo Calf Woman who promised to return when the world was again in crisis. She will then call for all races to come together to heal the earth and solve our mutual problems. (Photo: AP/Wide World Photos)

Chapter 12

❧ A new way to house-hunt ❧

"My plan is to reveal myself stage by stage,
and to draw together around me
those enlightened souls through whom I may work.
This process has begun, and soon, in my center,
my presence will become known."
—Maitreya

When I met with Maitreya in 1983, one of the last things he said to me was, "I hope you will remember to keep your promise to me that you have made this day." I had replied that I did not remember making any promises. He assured me that I had and that, when the time was right, the memory of my promise would be restored.

In 1995 I was living in Washington, DC and working for the United States Information Agency as a director of the Fulbright Scholarship Program. I enjoyed my position and planned to work at least another ten years for the government before even thinking of retiring. In August 1995, however, an unusual event took place, which gave me the first inkling that the Masters and I may have made other plans.

Knock three times to get my attention

It was a Saturday morning and I was vacuuming in my bedroom when I was suddenly struck by a strange jolt of energy between my eyes, in the eyebrow area.[1] I thought I had been hit by lightning or shocked by electricity as I slumped to the floor. An equally alarming possibility was that I had suffered a stroke, since the energy was focused in my head.

I was too confused to do anything except lie very still and collect my thoughts. As I lay there on the floor, wondering what had happened, I clearly heard a voice in my head say, "Sit down, close your eyes, and I will show you where you are going to live."[2]

I did not sit down *or* close my eyes. Clear as the message had been, I was more concerned about my health. I soon realized, however, that I was fine and sensed no lingering ill effects of whatever had just happened. Even so, I did consider going to the nearest emergency room to seek medical advice.

Second knock

Instead, I got up and, just as I was about to continue vacuuming, the same force seemed to strike me again between the eyebrows. Once more I heard a voice say, "Sit down and I will show you where you are going to live."

Although my conscious mind registered the message more clearly this time, my primary concern was again for my health. I checked myself for obvious symptoms of abnormal bodily functions like shaking hands, blurred vision, or unusual pain, but I found nothing out of the ordinary.

At the same time I was debating with myself about how to get to an emergency room to have the explosive feelings in my head investigated, I was also questioning these odd messages about a future place to live. It seemed that tomorrow or next week might be a more appropriate time to think about such things. I did not understand why I was having such banal thoughts at a time when my life might be in danger.

Third knock

Almost immediately I felt the force a third time, exactly as before, like a bolt of energy in the forehead between my eyes. Now clearer than before, the voice said, "Sit down *immediately* and I will show you where you are going to live."

This time I fell down on the sofa in my bedroom and closed my eyes, when I instantly had a vision of myself approaching a house.

I had no idea where the house was located or where this very realistic image could be coming from. I was, however, aware of a guide, a man who told me to look in certain directions and notice specific views. I have no memory of looking directly at him, but simply followed his instructions. It was like watching a color movie in which I was one of the characters.

A tour of my new home

First we entered the kitchen through the garage. The house was furnished, and I realized that the furniture looked just like my own. I saw a computer on a table in the kitchen corner and piles of papers on the dining room table. As we paused briefly at the entrance to the living room, I looked through the windows and saw a small patio garden, a high wall, and a pine tree beyond. I assumed there was a city street out there somewhere, but I couldn't see past the wall. Next my guide suggested we go upstairs to get a better view and visit what he said was the best room in the house.

At the top of the stairway was a large room with a series of windows at the far end. My guide pointed to them and said, "Look at this view—it faces east", as if facing east were in some way significant. I looked out the window and was puzzled by what I saw. Just as I had assumed, there was a street below, and beyond it a large open space with a brilliant green manicured lawn and pine trees.

The puzzling part was that beyond the lawn and the red tile rooftops of the houses on the other side, I saw a valley below a steep cliff or mountain range. There seemed to be no trees or greenery of any type growing in the valley or on the mountains. I assumed it was a desert, but couldn't understand how it could be so green by this house and so parched and barren just beyond. I had never seen anything like it, and I wondered where this place could possibly be.

I tried to see more of the valley by standing on my toes. Perhaps there was a river down there that kept things so green.

But my guide, obviously reading my thoughts, volunteered, "There is no river in the valley."

From windows on the opposite side of the house I could see a neat row of houses with red tile roofs and stucco siding. Directly beyond these houses was another strip of bright green lawn that rose gently uphill to where a second row of homes was perched. Beyond that there was nothing but clear, blue sky.

At this point my guide said, "You have now seen the house where you will live", and the adventure ended as abruptly as it had begun.

I opened my eyes and thought how strange the whole experience had been. By now I realized it had to be the work of one of the Masters. Although I didn't believe for a moment that I would ever live in such a place, I also knew the Masters do not waste their time and energy showing people things that are meaningless. I was intrigued but clueless.

A travel suggestion from parties unknown

In the weeks following the mysterious vision, life proceeded without incident. It was now September and I realized that, if I didn't take a vacation before the end of the year, I would forfeit my accumulated leave. I hurriedly began making plans to take ten days off in late October to go somewhere interesting with friends. But each time I put something together, it immediately fell apart.

Although nothing seemed to be working out, I was determined to get out of town and use all my leave, even if I had to go alone.

Since I had already scheduled the time off work, I couldn't change the dates, and the travel agent kept calling to remind me to purchase an airline ticket at least two weeks before my departure to avoid paying a higher fare. The Friday deadline was fast approaching, and I still didn't have a firm destination. In fact, on the morning of the last possible day, I was still calling friends, hoping for some miracle that would give me a great vacation.

At about noon, with only five hours remaining to purchase a ticket, I decided to call my friend Mike in Portland, Oregon. He and his wife had always wanted me to visit them, and for years had suggested that I would love Portland. Now, I thought, would be a good time to check it out. When I telephoned Mike at home, not having been in touch with him for well over a year, there was no answer. Then, just as I put down the receiver, the telephone rang. It was Mike! Another coincidence!

He said he was in Washington for the weekend and wanted to have lunch with me. I thought this would be the perfect opportunity to explain my plans and discuss things to do in the Portland area. Another hopeful scheme evaporated when Mike flatly stated that Portland was not my type of city. This reaction, coming as it did from a person who had always told me how much I would love the place, totally perplexed me.

Now that Portland was ruled out, I had to start again from scratch. With my dilemma unresolved, I returned to work, prepared to do some quick, last-minute thinking about travel possibilities.

When I stepped into my office, I couldn't believe what I saw. Scattered about on every flat surface—my desk, the floor, the chair seats, the tabletops, even the sofa—were travel pamphlets for Las Vegas, Nevada. I called in my secretary to find out who had been in my office, but she was equally surprised. No one had entered my office or even been at our end of the department, she said. Since her desk was located at the only entrance into or out of our suite of offices, it was unlikely that anyone could have gotten past her unnoticed.

We then went to my deputy's office thinking that, since her room was next to mine, she was either responsible for this display or knew who was. She knew nothing of the matter and, furthermore, had not left her office since before I went to lunch with Mike.

Determined to solve the mystery, I asked the travel agents downstairs if they had given Las Vegas pamphlets to anyone recently. Their reply was that they had only a few such brochures and hadn't distributed any in the past few days. I was now totally bewildered. How did all this travel literature about Las Vegas get into my office?

Finally, my deputy said, "Why don't you just go to Las Vegas on vacation? How bad could it be?"

I had never been to Las Vegas and had no interest in going there, but at this late date it appeared to be my only choice. I purchased a ticket within the hour, and two weeks later I was on my way to the desert mecca. How did I get into this situation? I felt pessimistic and a bit resentful about wasting my time, not to mention money, going to such a place. I'm sure the Masters had a chuckle or two knowing what was to come.

I arrive in Las Vegas

Things were bizarre from the moment I arrived. I had booked a room at the Sands Hotel, having read that Ronald and Nancy Reagan always stayed there when they visited the city. I also knew that Frank Sinatra and his friends spent a lot of time there during their show days. At least the Sands had some history going for it.

This legendary hotel had, however, lost my reservation, and other hotels in the city were booked solid with conventions. There was not a decent room anywhere, so when the Sands management offered to correct their mistake by giving me a large suite for the price of my original reservation, I gladly accepted.

It was opulent to say the least, with a full living room, dining room, kitchen, huge bedroom, the largest bar I have ever seen in a private room, and conveniently located next to the hotel pool. After a few days I adjusted to the size of the room and found it a great place to relax. The climate was perfect and the food fantastic. It was not long before I started enjoying myself in spite of being alone.

Sightseeing in Vegas

On the third day I rented a car to see more of the city and surrounding area. I had heard that Las Vegas was the fastest-growing city in America and wanted to see what that kind of growth looked like. I dropped into a real estate office that offered free maps.

One of the agents asked if I would like to visit some homes. I explained that I only wanted to see how the city was growing and had absolutely no interest in purchasing a home. He said he was about to view some new housing developments for prospective clients and would be happy to have me go along with him just for the company. He promised he would not try to sell me anything. This sounded interesting, so off we headed to the southeast section of the city.

He drove to a new development in Green Valley. We toured the model homes located along the east side of a golf course and spoke with a representative of the developer. I noticed nothing unusual about the community and was ready to move on, when the developer asked if we wanted to see the last available lot. My immediate reaction was no, but the agent who was driving said, "As long as we're here, why not?"

Since I was only a passenger, I tagged along as we drove to the far end of the property. I noticed that the wall surrounding the lot was completed but the house had not been started. Only the plumbing had been dug in, along with the water pipes. As we walked across the dry dirt floor I noticed a cement block, which I placed next to the wall.

Déjà vu at Green Valley

As the two agents chatted about the site, I stood on the block and peered over the wall. Across the street was a large grassy strip with houses at the end and dry hills on the far side of the valley.

I mused to myself, "It looks exactly the way I remember it." My logical mind instantly protested, "Remember what? What could you possibly remember?"

I had never been to Las Vegas, nor could I think of any place I had visited recently that looked anything like this. I could not understand why I had the distinct impression I had seen this view before. "Perhaps in a dream," I thought.

Then it came to me in a flash: this was the view I had seen six weeks ago in the strange vision. Here was the green park and, far beyond, the dry mountains of greater Las Vegas. It was not a fantasy after all, but a real place.

I recalled the words of the Master on that day, "Sit down and I will show you where you are going to live."

I turned and ran to the opposite side of the lot. The real estate agents probably thought I was crazy, but I was on a mission to verify every detail, to see if everything was just as I had seen it earlier. I heard nothing they said to me.

The green strip on the opposite side was a golf course, and the houses on higher ground above it were part of another development. There were the street, the houses, the strips of green grass, and the hills. There were the pine trees in the park and the larger homes on the far side. Everything appeared just the same.

I realized that when the house was finished the view would be perfect. I remember asking the developer what direction the house would face. When he said east, I knew I had to purchase this lot. Although I didn't know why an east-facing direction was important, I hadn't forgotten that the Master had made a point of it.

When we went back to the developer's office, I was still confused and wondered what all this meant. I thought about how the Master had managed to guide me to Las Vegas and then to this house as the first stop on the day's tour without arousing the tiniest suspicion in me. It seemed impossible, but it had happened. Everything seemed meticulously planned, and it all came together perfectly. Was this somehow connected with my earlier promise to Maitreya?

I become a homeowner

Now I had to make a decision. What would I do about the house? I could see no possible way of moving to Las Vegas in the foreseeable future. I had a job in Washington. If I resigned now, I would have no income to live on. Nevertheless, when the developer said that, for a small down payment, he would hold the house for me until it was completed, I said yes.

I figured it would take at least another six months for the construction to be completed, and I could use that time to decide whether I really wanted to buy the house. It would also give me some time to figure out what the Masters were up to.

The real estate agent who thought I was just along for the ride was shocked that I wanted to purchase the first house I visited, sight unseen. He insisted that we tour other houses, and I understood his reasoning completely. Since I was unwilling to tell him about my experience of seeing this particular house in a vision, I just played along and spent the next two days looking at houses, just to make him feel he had done his job responsibly.

Upon my return to Washington, colleagues were shocked at my uncharacteristically impulsive behavior. They could not understand why I would want to live so far away from Washington, and I felt I could not explain the extraordinary circumstances to them.

The next six months flew by and the house was completed right on schedule, but nothing had changed to make the move possible. Now I had to make an important decision solely on faith. I reasoned that, if the Masters wanted me to live in Las Vegas, they would find a way to make it happen. All I had to do was buy the house.

Waiting for a miracle

I did my part. I had the lawyers send the papers to my office. I signed and returned them and assumed ownership of the house. There was no celebration, just the nagging question as to whether I had done the right thing, especially since I would now have to sell my home in Washington.

Unfortunately, it was a time when real estate prices in the metropolitan area were rapidly collapsing. Although it was a bad time for sellers, I now had no choice. I hoped that my reasoning was right and my faith well placed. How would the Masters help me resolve this situation?

Chapter 13

᧞ Those who look for signs ᧞

"Those who search for signs will find them,
but my method of manifestation is more simple."
—Maitreya
"He is going to flood the world with such happenings
that the mind can never comprehend it."
—Maitreya's associate

As the months passed I became more confident that the house I had purchased in Las Vegas was the choice of the Master, but I also had to face reality: I now had two houses, two mortgages, and was still working in Washington without any visible way to retire—or the means to survive without a job.

So, having found a new home under such uncanny circumstances, I moved in with friends and simply waited for the next miracle to take place. I needed to unload the Washington mortgage, but there was not a buyer in sight. Not even one real estate agent had visited!

It was now June of 1996 and friends suggested that we visit a small Baptist church near Knoxville, Tennessee, that had miraculous 'crosses of light' appearing in its windows. It had been reported that crowds of people gathered every night to see this shimmering spectacle. I was definitely in the mood for a miracle, so we jumped in the car and headed for Knoxville.

Crosses of light

I first read about this mysterious phenomenon in *Share International*.[1] There it was reported than the first news story about crosses of light appeared in the *Pasadena Star News*

(Southern California) on May 27, 1988. A cross had appeared in El Monte, California, in the bathroom window of an apartment occupied by a Hispanic family.

Later, crosses of light were reported in other places around the world—usually in private homes—and thousands of people would flock to see them, many claiming to be healed. To me, the most spectacular crosses of light are those that appeared in the windows of the Copper Ridge Baptist Church in Knoxville. The story of these particular crosses became widely known in January of 1996 when CBS-TV aired a report.

The church has been there for over 135 years, yet there were now only 14 regular members. So, in November, 1995 Reverend Joe Bullard decided to retire from his ministry.

One evening early in November, however, he and his wife Mildred drove past the church and were amazed to see a radiant white light surrounding the entire building. They felt it was a sign to stay with the church. Then, on November 8th, as Reverend Bullard was giving the Sunday sermon, he noticed a peculiar light formation coming through the windows. The first cross of light appeared.

The unusual manifestation is made by a light source refracting through the type of glass commonly found in bathroom windows, forming a holographic image of an even-armed cross within a diamond. The image appears to be suspended in mid-air between glass and light. The light source is usually a light bulb, but it can also be a candle, street light, the sun or moon.

Reverend Bullard discovered that his crosses could be seen both during the daylight hours and at night when the lights within and without created images of crosses in every window of the church. Even more puzzling was the image in a back window, where five letters spelled the name of 'Jesus' in golden light.

Almost immediately after the discovery of the crosses, some members of this fundamentalist congregation objected to opening the church to the public, but Reverend Bullard believed it was a sign from God to heal people and insisted the church must remain open to all.

In an interview with *Share International* reporter Buddy Piper, Reverend Bullard recalled other unexplained happenings since the crosses had appeared:[2]

"My board members and I have had some strange assurances that something is really going on. One night, before people came to see the crosses, we were sitting on one side of the church, when several of us saw a tall man wearing a turban appear on the opposite side of the church and walk slowly forward next to the wall. He was absolutely perfect in form. Two other people then appeared who had more of a cloudy appearance, and they followed him forward. Every couple of steps the last person in line turned slightly toward us and waved in a friendly manner.

"When they reached the front of the church they turned around, and we expected to see the two followers leading the way back, but the first man was again in front and the others followed, as before. When they had made the walk three times, they disappeared. That certainly caught the attention of some of our members. They're still telling everybody about it!

"And then I got another experience. I had to go to the bathroom one night and, on my way back to bed, a small cross appeared in the room and I heard a voice say, 'Keep those church doors open and it won't be long till I will be back.' I said, 'Who are you?' Then the cross and the voice disappeared. I thought I was losing my mind for a minute."

Many people claimed healings, others reported seeing 'angels', and still others saw strange markings that resembled a cherub's footprint permanently impressed on one of the windowsills. Thousands of people said they experienced some miracle while looking at these crosses.

My own Tennessee miracle

When I visited the church that evening in June 1996, I was amazed to see that the crosses appeared white during the day but golden at night. I also noticed they were not the shape of the Christian cross or crucifix. Rather, they were 'even-armed', a symbol for the Aquarian age and belonging to people of all religions and of no religion. As I stood inside the church looking out through the windows, the crosses, suspended in space between the window and the street lamp providing the light source, seemed to be 30 feet or more in height.

I spoke at length with Reverend Bullard, who told me in great detail about the crosses and all the related miracles. As we were about to leave he asked me, "Do *you* require a miracle?"

I said, "Well, in fact, I do. I need to sell my home in Washington."

Bullard led me to a large book and explained that many people who visited the crosses of light had their requests answered after they recorded them and signed their names in this book. He explained that he knew this was so because many people wrote to him afterwards, saying that their request had been answered in some miraculous way. I could see no harm in asking for a miracle and added my name to the ledger.

On Sunday morning we left for Washington. When I arrived home late that afternoon, I had a phone call from the real estate agent who told me a miracle had taken place. While I had been driving back from Knoxville, not one, but three couples had visited my home. All three wanted to buy it immediately. I was stunned, thinking that just the previous night I had asked for this miracle.

I sold the house to the couple who wanted to pay cash. Then I packed my personal belongings, including my furniture, and shipped them to Las Vegas where my new house stood completed but empty. I flew to Las Vegas, set up the basic household effects, locked the doors, and returned to Washington. Almost everything I owned was now in Las Vegas, except me.

It was August of 1996, and I was living with friends and going to work as usual. Fortunately, my friends tolerated my crazy decision and placed no limits on my stay. I had no idea how long I would be living with this arrangement, but still felt confident that, when the time was right, I would be able to move to Las Vegas.

Other signs of Maitreya's presence

Sadly, the congregation in the Knoxville church was unwilling to receive so many visitors and finally took severe measures: they relieved Reverend Bullard of his duties and boarded up the church windows, ultimately removing them, bringing to an end one of the most extraordinary manifestations of divine intervention I have ever known. In other places, however, these crosses of light have been treated with the respect they are due and continue to radiate their healing energy to thousands of people who come to see them.

I firmly believe that Maitreya and the Masters of Wisdom are creating such miracles worldwide to re-awaken humanity's aspiration and anticipation of a 'further revelation', which can occur when we show the necessary readiness. I also believe that Maitreya, from his high vantage point, sees that humanity *is* ready and that the time for his appearance is now.

Each week the news carries word of more and more unexplained phenomena occurring all over the world. The sheer volume of reports has caused major American news organizations to conduct polls and produce stories (including cover stories) such as: "In Search of the Sacred", "The Message of Mircles", "The New Age of Angels", "Do You Believe in Miracles", "The Case of the Weeping Madonna", "Waiting for the Messiah", and "The Meaning of Mary". Millions of people can now lay claim to their own personal miracle, and even the scientific community is taking these events more seriously. People are beginning to realize that such a proliferation of miracles must be the work of some force or law beyond the ordinary.

In 1988, shortly before the trend began to escalate, *Share International* magazine published these words: "Maitreya is going to flood the world with such happenings that the mind can never comprehend it."[3]

There is so much information on these miraculous events that it would require a tome to do the topic justice. I can relate only a few such stories in this chapter. What I wish to show is that these miracles are universal. They have occurred within all the major religious groups of the world and outside the religious community as well. Let's take a look at some of these miracles.

Milk-drinking Hindu statues[4]

The Hindu world was shaken in the fall of 1995, when statues of the elephant god Ganesha appeared to 'drink' the milk offerings. Presenting a spoonful of milk to a statue representing an aspect of God is a customary part of Hindu religious practice. On September 21st, however, the statues of marble and bronze responded in an extraordinary way—the milk simply vanished!

It started in a temple on the outskirts of Delhi, India, when milk offered to a statue of Ganesha disappeared from the spoon.

Reports of the miracle flashed across the globe. Hindu temples in India, England, North America, Singapore, Hong Kong, Australia and elsewhere soon reported the same mysterious phenomenon.

The faithful flooded into Hindu temples around the world to see for themselves if statues were really drinking milk. Shortages of milk were soon reported in India, and police were called in to control the crowds. Alerted by reports on CNN, temples in Los Angeles, San Francisco and New York reported that their statues of Ganesha were also drinking milk.

It became a global event eagerly covered by television, radio, and newspapers. Journalists were humbled when they too had the statues of gods drinking from their milk-filled spoons. Skeptics proclaimed it a giant hoax, but as one Indian corporate executive told the Indian news agency, "It cannot be a hoax. Where would all that milk being offered go?"

Despite the evidence, some people still refused to believe that a miracle had occurred. However, the five-day phenomenon created hope and expectancy among Hindus that something positive and significant was about to happen in the world. Vedic scholars poring over sacred scriptures found ancient references that statues drinking milk would be one of the signs that "a Great Soul had descended".

Appearances of the Blessed Virgin

In the past few years, many statues of Mary, mother of Jesus, have been found weeping tears or shedding blood or fragrant oils, and images of the Blessed Mother have been appearing on trees, buildings and other surfaces. Many apparitions of saints and angels have also been documented. These reports will be familiar to most Christians, and certainly to Roman Catholics.

"The Search for Mary", *Time* magazine's year-end cover story in 1991, examined the worldwide revival of faith in the Virgin

Mary and the reports of her increasing appearances in recent years. The traditional apparition sites of Lourdes in France, Fatima in Portugal, and Guadalupe in Mexico are some of the most famous. In the past 20 years, however, several new sites have received media coverage, chief among these the village of Medjugorje in Bosnia, where a group of children has had daily discussions with the Blessed Mother since 1981.

In America there have been many sightings of Mary, including the glowing apparition which appears each morning on the blue tiles in a church in Santa Ana, California. In Clearwater, Florida, people flock to see a two-story-high shimmering image of the Virgin, which covers the glass siding of an office building. The image cannot be removed, even when scrubbed with chemicals, and renewed *itself* after vandals defaced the glass surface.

Mary is also seen weeping. Sometimes it is a painting or icon but, more often, it is a statue that weeps tears of blood, water or oil. These fluids, collected on pieces of cotton or cloth, are said to have the power to heal the sick. One of these weeping statues is located in central Las Vegas, Nevada.

Las Vegas, Nevada—1993

The weeping Virgin of Las Vegas is not as well known as some other Marian phenomena, but it is an example of a privately-owned statue that weeps on specific holidays.[5] A copy of the statue of Our Lady of Guadalupe in Mexico, it is owned by a Hispanic family in Las Vegas and is housed in a shrine the family built for her in the backyard.

The statue wept for the first time on May 31, 1993, and the local CBS television affiliate sent a camera crew to record the event. The statue was removed from its pedestal to prove that it wasn't a hoax. When the statue was replaced, it wept for the camera crew, as if on cue. The tears were collected in cotton balls to be shared with the faithful, who soon discovered the tears had miraculous powers. Many claimed to be cured from a variety of illnesses including cancer. But tears are not the only miracle manifested by the Las Vegas Madonna. At her feet is the bust of a small angel that regularly sweats a fragrant, rose-scented oil from its face and hair.

In October 1993, while 32 people knelt in prayer before the statue, another miracle took place. It was a very windy day, but suddenly the wind died down and the clouds broke. Members of the prayer group noticed the image of the Guadalupe Madonna forming in the sky. The glowing rays of the sun created the appearance of a spiked, golden aura typical of such statues.

The Las Vegas Madonna statue wept for the second time on December 12, 1993, the feast day of Our Lady of Guadalupe, and the anniversary of her appearance to Juan Diego, a poor Aztec Indian.[6]

Another miracle took place on September 25, 1995. Not only did the Madonna weep tears during that event, but an even-armed cross appeared on her forehead, similar to a raised scar.

The bishop of Las Vegas called this local phenomenon a fake. Fear continues to plague the Catholic church in such matters; it does not know how to respond to so many miraculous claims being attributed to the Madonna. Nevertheless, for those who have experienced her presence and healing through this statue, no external confirmation is needed.

The name of Allah—1997

To Muslims, Allah is the name of God, so it has inspired some awe that this name has been mysteriously appearing, spelled out in Arabic script on eggs, on beans, and even inside vegetables being prepared for consumption in Muslim homes.[7] In London, England, when an eggplant was sliced open, the seeds inside formed the Arabic script for 'Ya-Allah', meaning Allah exists.

In Holland, merchant Mikail Güçlü noticed that the eggs he had just purchased in the market had misshapen shells. Upon closer examination, it appeared these irregularities were forming the Arabic letters for Allah, so he called to consult a friend with better knowledge of script. They discovered that the eggshells had formed ridges to spell out the message, "There is but one God, Allah, and Mohammed is his prophet." The men took the eggs to the local mosque to show the Imam, or high priest. Everyone present agreed they had correctly interpreted the script.

Several days after purchasing the unusual eggs, Güçlü was sorting beans when he discovered he had 500 grams worth, all bearing the name of Allah. The miracle beans were given to the mosque, where they were cooked and shared with the congregation. About 40 people enjoyed a complete meal from this pound of beans, and there was still some left. According to the article in *Share International* magazine, the Imam said: "We could serve as much as we wished, and the supply was still not exhausted."

In various parts of the Islamic world, where statues and images are not allowed, there have been reports of the name Allah appearing not only on fruits and vegetables, but even on the belly fur of lambs and goats.

White buffalo—1994

If Christians have crosses of light and weeping statues of the Madonna, the long-awaited birth of a white buffalo represents a similar sign from the Great Spirit to Native Americans. It is not only a good omen but also the most significant of prophetic signs.

The odds of such a birth are said to be about six million to one. Yet, in the last decade, four such calves have been born, symbolizing for Native Americans the return of the White Buffalo Calf Woman, a legendary figure who came at a time when the people were in great suffering. When she departed she promised to return when the world was again in crisis. She will call for all races to come together to heal the earth and solve our mutual problems.[8] Some believe the original prophecy has been fulfilled, as they have already seen her. Like the Masters, she is said to appear in many guises.

Red heifer—1997

Some Jews are hailing the birth of a red heifer in Israel as a sign from God that the Messiah is near. The rust-colored calf is of a variety believed extinct for centuries. The ninth such birth in Israel is thought to have taken place in 70 AD. According to the 12th century Jewish philosopher, Maimonides, the 10th and final red heifer will be discovered by the Messiah.[9]

Buddhist images appear—1987-2000

In 1987, an image of the Bodhisattva, or future Buddha, appeared like a cross of light in a window in Nagano City, Japan. Emanating rainbow-colored light, this lovely image was soon followed by a second image on a wall. That image, which had plainly visible eyes, wore a pointed hat, held a water pot and sat on a lotus. In 1989, a third image of the Coming One appeared on another wall of the same house. Solid-looking, it seemed to float off the wall. The images have drawn hundreds of people to the home-shrine, many of whom have reported physical and psychological healings. The woman of the house suddenly acquired an ability to diagnose and heal illnesses and planned to spend the rest of her life helping others.[10]

As reported in 1999, a statue of Shakyamuni Buddha in Lhasa, Tibet cried real pearls. The frequent crying of these pearl tears by the statue was very moving to those who witnessed it. The manifestation of the pearls was attributed to Maitreya.[11]

In 2000, a sunset photograph taken by a passenger in a plane over Nara, Japan, produced, not the sunset, but a stunning image of Kannon, the Goddess of Compassion. A revered, religious figure, Kannon (or Kuan Yin in Chinese) is to Buddhism what the Blessed Mother is to Catholicism and is honored in almost every home in Japan and China. According to legend, Kannon is an enlightened Bodhisattva, or Buddha-to-be, who has chosen to retain human form until all the people achieve enlightenment.[12]

On the verge of a new revelation

It appears to me that Maitreya has found unique ways to send a message of hope to people of all faiths, preparing them for his imminent appearance by using the sacred images, artifacts and symbols familiar to each.

For those who believe he comes at this crucial time in history to liberate humanity and show us a new and better way to live, these miracles are among the many signs that he draws nearer every day. All people, irrespective of creed or belief, long for and expect some form of new revelation of essential truth. The miracles re-awaken this aspiration and spirit of anticipation.

Despite the apparent shortcomings of humanity, Maitreya has said we *are* ready to positively respond to his call. In numerous messages he has given to the world, he expresses confidence that we will accept his guidance and show both willingness and enthusiasm to change our world for the better. This time the Christ will remain with us for the entire age of Aquarius, some 2,250 years, as friend and teacher, working openly in our midst. He will show us how to live together as brothers and sisters, sharing the earth's resources.

We stand now on the verge of receiving this new revelation *directly* from the Teacher, without distortion and misinterpretation by others. Contrary to some popular views, I believe we are meant to *enjoy* our life experience on this planet, and Maitreya will show us how to achieve the greatest fulfillment of our divine heritage. Be aware, be awakened, and be ready for his call to action.

Chapter 14

❧ The Master at Medjugorje ❧

"The visionary Vicka promises that
miraculous healings will happen spontaneously
all over the world when the promised
'permanent sign' occurs at Medjugorje."
—The Visions of the Children

"On that day [of declaration] ... hundreds of thousands
of miraculous healings will take place
throughout the world."
—Benjamin Creme

I first heard the amazing story of Medjugorje during a lecture by Janice T. Connell, author of several books on the miracles and the teachings of the Blessed Mother in Medjugorje.[1] Jan befriended the visionaries and held numerous interviews with them and their families. Over the years Jan and I became better acquainted, and I attended numerous public meetings where she discussed the meaning of these events and their importance to the world.

She is devoted to the Blessed Mother[2] in a way that few of us can comprehend. In fact, one might say she has a special relationship of her own with the Blessed Mother. Although she is shy about discussing it, many people have publicly witnessed extraordinary events at her lectures.

Signs of a Master's presence

Medjugorje is an excellent example of how the Masters create a focal point to heighten humanity's anticipation of something that is about to happen. Such miraculous events have helped them to enlighten millions of Catholics worldwide and to prepare them for the coming of Maitreya (the Christ to the Christians) in a manner they can understand and accept.

Since 1981, the messages from this small Bosnian village have had a profound effect on much of the Western Christian world and galvanized it like no other event since the apparitions at Fatima. In Medjugorje, the image of a beautiful lady is said to have appeared more that 3,500 times over the years.

Some believe that what is happening in Medjugorje could well be the most important event in the history of the Catholic church since the Day of Pentecost. Even the pope has spoken positively about the messages the visionaries receive from the Blessed Mother.

Millions of pilgrims, Christian and non-Christian, religious and non-religious, have visited this remote village to see for themselves the place where so many have claimed miraculous cures from illness or simply found an inner peace that had been absent in their lives. Whatever these pilgrims found in Medjugorje, few were disappointed with their visit.

Similar messages from the Blessed Mother and Maitreya

Having read some of the teachings from Maitreya[3], I decided to compare them with the messages from the Blessed Mother. Both sources offer important insights into our changing times and spiritual understanding, and they share many similar views, although this may at first be obscured by the differences in terminology.

The messages delivered by the visionaries of Medjugorje are aimed primarily at Christians, using words that are familiar to them. They speak to an audience that understands God from the vocabulary of religion. The Blessed Mother speaks often of sharing and recognizing the God within. If she has one overriding message, it might be to focus more on prayer, fasting, trusting totally in God and being free of fear.

Maitreya's messages are aimed at the worldwide community—religious and non-religious alike—and use the language of philosophy, psychology and science. If Maitreya has one message that could be called his 'signature philosophy', it might be, "Be who you are" and practice "honesty of mind, sincerity of spirit and detachment".

The words of both the Blessed Mother and Maitreya are deceptively simple, yet convey profound truths which can be adapted to any level of human understanding.

We are all conditioned from birth by our experiences and, therefore, we cannot expect that everyone will see the world in the same way or extract the same meaning from the teachings. Fortunately, the Masters dispense their wisdom in an infinite variety of ways, and we are only asked to accept what has the ring of truth for us.

Following are a few examples of similar views expressed in different terms, and include clarifications from the visionaries themselves.

Conversion and self-awareness

When asked for the meaning of the word 'conversion', one visionary said, "Conversion is awareness that we live before the face of God day and night"[4], which might also be understood as: the awareness that God is within us brings conversion. Another visionary said, "Each person created by God has access to God in the silence of his heart."

Jiddu Krishnamurti, one of the most well-known and respected spiritual teachers of the 20th century, who many believe was a disciple of Maitreya, said, in effect, that Self-awareness (or conversion) is the first step toward Self-realization, and Self-realization is the goal of our human experience. Thus, awareness of God within is conversion (or Self-awareness) and leads to Self-realization or God-consciousness within the human form. Each is a necessary step in the evolutionary process.[5]

Prayer and fear

Messages from the Blessed Mother implore everyone to pray from their hearts. This may be something more than ordinary prayer—perhaps a learned skill—as the visionaries report that, after years of repeating this message, the Blessed Mother is still disappointed that people have not *learned* how to pray.

We have a clue to 'prayer from the heart' when visionary Marija said, "The first condition for any effective prayer group is to put away all fear from your heart forever." Thus, freedom from fear and effective prayer are closely related.

Both Maitreya and Krishnamurti focus on the problem of fear in humanity and clearly state that fear ceases to exist in the presence of love. There can be no Self-realization with fear. Total attention dispels fear.

Biblically speaking, I John 4:18 says, "In love there is no room for fear, but perfect love drives out fear, because fear implies punishment and no one who is afraid has come to perfection in love."

Therefore, what I am hearing in the messages from both Maitreya and the Blessed Mother is that, if we are to place our trust in God completely and become Self-realized souls, we must abandon fear. No halfway attempt is useful. One must be completely free of fear to experience God, by whatever name we call Him.

Prayer from the heart and meditation

The Medjugorje visionaries suggest that 'prayer from the heart' is so important in our lives that we must learn to pray constantly until we are praying 24 hours a day—a state of continuous prayer. They do not give many clues about how to do this, but Krishnamurti makes it somewhat clearer when he writes something similar about meditation—not the meditation understood by most people, but a meditation (prayer) as "the correct observation of life". We could also refer to it as "unprejudiced observation".

Krishnamurti sums it up best when he says, "Meditation is the understanding of life, the life everyday with all its complexity, misery, sorrow, loneliness, despair, the drive to become famous, successful, the fear, envy—to understand all *that* is meditation."

No man can understand himself (Self-realization) without using this knowledge. Thus, says Krishnamurti, "Meditation [correct prayer] is the way of life, every day, every hour and every minute." It is a state of being that all of us must achieve if we hope to create the world Maitreya, the Christ, envisions for us.

Achieving a state of constant prayer

How, one may ask, does this state of perpetual meditation or constant prayer happen? When Maitreya tells us to practice honesty of mind, I believe it is what Krishnamurti refers to as correct observation of life. If we realize that the human thinking process distorts the reality we observe daily, we can begin to understand these messages better. Man observes "what should be" (desires or fears) instead of "what is" (facts or reality), says Krishnamurti. In other words, Maitreya's "honesty of mind" is Krishnamurti's "observation without prejudice" and living with that fact. Anything else leads to hypocrisy.

Krishnamurti also says, "Meditation is observation when the observer is not." The observer who allows the past knowledge stored in his brain to interfere with the observation process suffers from a prejudiced mind. Man has always preferred to live in the past (his ideas) and not the present reality (what is). He finds it difficult to live in the present, the now. The observer, we are told, can only see the fact (reality) with a quiet mind. When he learns not to feed his past knowledge (prejudices) into his present observation, he can see clearly the fact (what is). Then, by wholly observing "what is", the sense of being a separate observer disappears, and pure observation remains. This is a quiet or open-minded state—a rarity in today's world.

Krishnamurti goes even further in trying to make this matter clear by linking it to daily living and correct morality. He explains that when we understand correct meditation, we bring order to our lives. When we have order in our lives, we also have true morality. It comes; we do not have to seek it. Although 'social morality', which is nothing more than respectability, is actually immoral, *true* morality is bringing order both within oneself and without. Always live with the fact (reality), nothing else, he tells us. Give attention to the fact and you will have energy in abundance; you will live without fear. It is this energy that will keep your mind clear. It is love—not ideas, not sentiment, not emotions—but love. This is the morality born of the divine Self.

Thus, I believe this meditation (non-prejudiced observation) is the same as prayer from the heart as spoken of by Our Lady of Medjugorje.

Although I am giving you only a brief outline of the teachings, it is enough for you to understand that we are being offered a new road map to search for who we truly are. This knowledge is not the sole possession of any one group or teacher. It is being offered in many ways so that people have the opportunity to hear it in a form that rings true in their hearts.

Fasting and detachment

Why is fasting important in the messages from Medjugorje? Visionary Ivanka said, "[The Blessed Mother] says a person who does not fast does not know God" and "...her children must fast with their eyes, their tongue, their hands, their feet, their ears...These experiences [fasting] free us from attachments that are transitory."

Freedom from attachments is another way of saying *detachment*. Maitreya also speaks about detachment: "Honesty of mind, sincerity of spirit, and detachment should apply to all your actions." According to Maitreya, detachment is the process whereby man ceases to identify with the body, mind and spirit, for to so identify is to be attached to earthly things. Anything performed with detachment is divine. If it is divine, it does not cling to body, mind or spirit.

Again, the teachings seem to correspond. Fasting with our eyes, tongue, hands, feet and ears is a way of telling us to free ourselves from desires—to practice detachment. Do not, however, make the mistake of thinking that detachment from material things means removing ourselves from them physically. Detachment means living in the material world but remaining detached mentally.

A permanent sign and the Day of Declaration

Many interesting parallels exist between descriptions of Maitreya's Day of Declaration and the messages from the Blessed Mother. Both tell us we can expect a major spiritual event that will shake the world. This event, according to the apparitions of the Blessed Mother, will change humanity. Both say it can be easy or difficult depending upon humanity itself. If we decide to change the way we live, we will enter a great and glorious age with relative ease. If we refuse to change our ways, the transition will be difficult and many will suffer. What then is this great event?

A permanent sign

The visionary children, now young adults, guard ten secrets that will be revealed on that special day. They say this event, and a special sign on the mountaintop near Medjugorje, accompanied by miraculous healings worldwide, will convince all doubters. This sign has been described as indestructible, something we have never seen before. As I understand the messages, ten days before this monumental spiritual event, the visionaries from Medjugorje will notify their priest, who will pray and fast for seven days and then announce the secrets to the entire world. We will then have only days to prepare.

The Day of Declaration

Likewise, those following the emergence of Maitreya are waiting for a very special day called the Day of Declaration, which will be like a second Pentecost.

On that day, Maitreya will appear on worldwide television. His words of inspiration will telepathically sound in every person's mind—in their own language. His energy of Love will enter the hearts of all, galvanizing humanity to save the world, and hundreds of thousands of spontaneous healings will occur.

I firmly believe that this Day of Declaration is the same event that is promised by the apparition at Medjugorje. It will be the day on which humanity will be introduced to the Spiritual Kingdom, the day when Christians will recognize the reappearance of the Christ in a physical body walking among them, and also the day when those of other traditions will know their awaited Teacher has returned.

Tired of waiting

1981, the year the apparitions at Medjugorje began, seems like the distant past to believers looking for the grand spiritual event to take place as promised by the visionaries. Many have grown weary of waiting. Likewise, many who expect the appearance of Maitreya and the Masters of Wisdom question the 'delay'.

Lack of patience is a prominent human trait, especially in the Western world where time is considered money. We want what we want now, without further delay, and easily lose faith if our expectations are not met. We begin to doubt what we may have so strongly believed earlier.

What we don't really comprehend yet is that, in the Spiritual Kingdom, the realm of the Masters and initiates of the world, there is no time. All things are in the present, the now. What is for us still a future event has already occurred as far as they are concerned, but may not yet have 'precipitated down' to our level of awareness. But the signposts are there, if we care to read them.

For one thing, we can look at the dramatic and positive changes that have taken place in the world since Maitreya's arrival in London in 1977 and the Blessed Mother's first appearance at Medjugorje in 1981.

Since then, more and more of us have been willing to admit that we are living life in contradiction to our spiritual nature by saying one thing and then doing the opposite, often using the word of God to harm and insult our fellow human beings.

But very slowly a measure of peace and goodwill is percolating into our consciousness, and we are coming to understand that the needs of our neighbors, nation and world are as important as our own. When Maitreya is certain we truly want to live as one human family, he will complete his emergence into full public view, and the promise of the Blessed Mother in Medjugorje will be fulfilled.

Telling the story

In the meantime, a small but growing number of people continue to share the story of the emergence, and the flood of miracles keeps humanity in a state of wonderment. Gradually, as more people have their own personal experience of the Masters, as has been my privilege, skepticism will give way to conviction, and conviction to everyday reality.

Chapter 15

ᔌ Las Vegas or bust ᔍ

"I am indeed among you in a new way:
your brothers and sisters know me,
have seen me, and call me friend and brother."
—Maitreya

After selling my Washington home and moving in with friends I saw no sign as to how or when I might become a permanent resident of Las Vegas. I invited my mother and sister to join me for Christmas to see the new house. They loved the house, but in Las Vegas? This gave me a few days to unpack some extra boxes and arrange furniture, and I took the opportunity to further acquaint myself with the city. I decided it ranked high among the more bizarre and strange places I have visited in the world. We had a lovely Christmas and, after taking a few extra days of vacation to make it a long holiday, I flew back to my job in Washington. I had now spent enough time in Las Vegas to know that it was a city where I could feel comfortable and confident that family and friends would visit often.

Upon my return to the office, my deputy welcomed me with, "You won't believe this. Congress has just offered the agency the option to allow some officers to retire early and receive immediate retirement benefits. Not only that," she added, "but everyone approved for this special offer will receive a $25,000 departure bonus if they leave by the end of the pay period."

This sounded like the miracle I had been waiting for and had the unmistakable quality of 'Masters at work'. The offer was, however, limited to a certain number of management-level personnel, and my friends in the office thought my chances were slim. I, on the other hand, was quite confident it would happen for me. Within a few days, I received word that I had indeed been approved, and the entire process of negotiating early retirement, completing the paper work and packing up my office all took place within four days.

I wrapped up my duties and vacated the office by the end of the pay period as required. Although it was an enormous undertaking, it had all worked so fast and so smoothly that I was still in shock when retirement day arrived. I was now free to leave Washington and move to my new home in Las Vegas.

I knew this had all happened with a hand from the Masters. What I still find amazing, though, is how subtly they work. Throughout this life-altering process, they never told me more than I needed to know for the moment at hand, a strategy not unlike that in government service!

Since I had shipped my household belongings to Nevada five months earlier, I had to move only my automobile and clothing. My ties to the area were now broken, with the exception of good friends.

I informed my temporary housing hosts that I now planned to drive to Las Vegas as soon as possible and start my new life. I'm sure they were dumbfounded by my urgent desire to leave so quickly. After all, I had been a resident of Washington for many years and had developed many attachments. Nevertheless, my friends were gracious, as usual, not only in offering me a place to live but also in supporting my curious wish to get to Nevada. They simply, and understandably, did not comprehend my interest in the Masters and the sense of positive anticipation I was feeling about my own future role in this great unfolding emergence of Hierarchy.

A drive to remember

In mid-January 1997 I packed the car with my last few possessions for the drive to Las Vegas. Knowing I did not want to drive alone cross-country in winter, my good friend Rudy offered to accompany me and take a flight back home. So he arranged for a few days leave from his job at the Department of Justice. Little did we know that a huge winter storm would begin sweeping across the nation on the very day we decided to head west.

I assumed that the southern route across Tennessee, Arkansas, New Mexico and Arizona would be safest in the winter. As it turned out, ordinary rain or snow would have been a blessing compared to the freezing rain, sleet, ice, snow and wind we encountered all the way to Las Vegas.

From the moment we departed Washington in the unanticipated storm, almost every mile along the way we witnessed overturned vehicles, truck accidents, and autos sliding off the interstate. Seeing this would have convinced any sane person to return to Washington and wait out the storm. But, for whatever reason, I felt the need to push on regardless of the potential dangers.

Always believing it was going to get better, we slowly drove through Virginia, where the road was so covered with snow we had no idea if we were actually on the highway or not. Overturned tractor-trailer trucks in ditches became a common sight. Cars disappeared off the highway, sliding down steep slopes of snow-covered grass as we watched dumbfounded.

Our worst fears realized

When we reached Tennessee, I thought the situation might improve, as the snow began to recede and the highway was again visible. My relief was short-lived. Soon, we were driving through an ice storm and, somewhere near Nashville, our worst road fears were realized.

Driving west at 50 miles per hour on Interstate 70, we saw signs warning of a steep downhill grade several miles long. I slowed down as we entered a fog bank that descended over our car. For a full minute I could see nothing beyond the hood and reduced my speed even more. Within half a mile the road dropped again sharply and, with that, the fog lifted high enough for us to see further ahead. The sight revealed was terrifying, and I tried not to panic.

Several hundred feet before us was a 'knot' of autos, trucks, vans and trailers all smashed together and gliding down the hill, mostly sideways. It looked like bumper cars at the county fair. We could see other autos and trucks being pushed off the highway by this mass of vehicles, which continued to slide down the steep grade and, at the same time, slowly turn like a giant pinwheel that spanned the entire highway.

To make matters worse, the vehicles being pushed off the highway fell 30-40 feet down a deep ravine, landing on the cars at the bottom. I saw no way to avoid a serious crash—or maybe even death.

We start to slide

I gently pressed the brake pedal. The car spun around 45 degrees so we too were now sliding down the hill sideways—on a sheet of ice. There was absolutely nothing for the tires to grab.

I looked out my side window up the hill and saw a tractor-trailer rig heading straight for us. It was gaining speed, and I knew this huge truck was about to crush my little car into the spinning mass of vehicles below. I envisioned Rudy and myself imprisoned lifelessly in a car that looked like a pancake.

I tried desperately to change our course, but turning the steering wheel accomplished nothing. We glided helplessly toward the compacted mass of vehicles sliding downhill, with the occasional car breaking lose and falling completely off the highway.

We ask the Masters for help

I warned my hapless companion to brace himself for a crash and suggested, with no lack of urgency in my voice, "Rudy, now is the time to ask the Masters for help."

Immediately, without any effort on my part, the car righted itself and headed down the road facing forward. I informed Rudy I was no longer steering the car.

Trying to look at the bright side, we agreed that going forward was good since the engine of the car might protect us from the frontal impact, but there was still the matter of this huge truck barreling down the road behind us. I had no idea what cargo it might be carrying or if it would flip over and kill us on the spot. I looked again at the vehicles in front. We were only a few feet away from impact. Then it happened—a true miracle.

Miraculous intervention

The spinning mass of vehicles started to separate and, without my aid, our car headed straight for the opening. My body was frozen in place; I could only stare in disbelief as the miracle unfolded. As we proceeded, this huge lump of crumpled metal gradually parted for us, like the biblical opening of the Red Sea.

As the vehicles moved around us, there appeared to be no more than an inch or two of clearance. I had time to make this observation since I was certainly not steering the car. In seconds we were on the other side moving straight down the hill as if nothing had happened.

I looked behind me and watched the 'path' close just moments after we emerged safely. Then, the tractor-trailer plowed into the heap of vehicles we had just passed through, creating even more havoc.

I told Rudy we could not stop and offer assistance since the car would not slow down. It appeared to have a mind of its own. We later heard reports on the radio that many dozens of vehicles were involved in this pile-up on the Tennessee interstate.

Bending the laws of physics

Although the 'parting of the metal' was enough of a miracle, I believe it was an even greater miracle that actually saved us. I vividly remember that, as my car entered the opening mass of spinning autos, we were 'entombed' in the center. While the other vehicles were turning in unison around us, my car moved in a straight line directly down the highway.

At one point I looked down at the road surface because I was sure the auto beside me was entering my vehicle. I waited for the sound of metal on metal but there was no noise—only an eerie silence. Then I looked back toward my rear fender because there was another auto spinning directly into it. Again, no metal-on-metal noise and, in fact, no damage to my car whatsoever.

I am convinced that something other than normal physics took place. We should have been caught and crushed along with those other vehicles, but we were not. From my line of sight the autos around us should have at least scraped the sides of my car, but they did not. What then was happening?

I know that the Masters can be especially helpful to and protective of someone working with them. *How* they do it is often the great mystery. I am convinced that my vehicle did, in fact, collide with those others on the highway, but somehow the physical universe did something extraordinary.

Helena Blavatsky, the co-founder of the Theosophical Society who introduced the Masters to Western audiences, wrote about a similar incident that happened to her while she rode in a carriage in New York City. As her carriage and another were about to collide, they simply passed through each other and all was well. Apparently, at the subatomic level particles have different properties and can behave in ways we do not yet understand. I still search my mind for a complete explanation.

We arrive safely in Las Vegas

Tennessee was not our last bout with treacherous weather; even the windy semi-deserts of New Mexico were covered with snow and ice that winter. Nevertheless, we arrived in one piece in Las Vegas at 3:00 a.m. on the morning of the fourth day and went straight to bed. When we awoke, we heard on the news that all roads to the city were closed due to snow at the higher elevations. Tourists who had driven to Las Vegas from Phoenix and Los Angeles were stranded for several days until the roads were reopened. It was then that my friend Rudy and I realized how extremely fortunate we were to have traveled safely for those three days.

I have no explanation for this extraordinary sequence of events which saved our lives, except my conviction that we are all, in many ways, protected by unseen forces throughout our lives. If we are spared injury or death by some miraculous intervention, we might attribute it to our 'guardian angel' or to angels in general. I suggest that what we experience as angels are, instead, the Masters of Wisdom performing one of their many helpful functions in relation to humanity. Sometimes they work behind the scenes and sometimes they appear as ordinary people coming to our aid.

Whether we accept it or not, whether we know of their existence or not, the Masters are protecting us, so long as it does not interfere with our soul's plan. They know precisely when they are allowed to intervene in our lives and when they may not. It is a comforting thought to know that we are never alone.

Chapter 16

✤ Promises to keep ✤

"Many there are whom I call.
Many there are who wait and listen.
Few there are, indeed, who seize the time and act.
These few are my people.
May you become one of them."
—Maitreya

On a visit to Los Angeles in 1998, I encountered Maitreya and one of the Masters of Wisdom on the sidewalk on Rodeo Drive in Beverly Hills. This may appear to be a strange place to see the Masters, until one realizes they are 'out and about' everywhere, missing no opportunity to help, teach or inspire. In my case another lesson was brewing.

I had recently moved to Las Vegas where I was totally without family or friends. My nearest friends were in Los Angeles, so I was thrilled to be spending the weekend with them and having an opportunity for pleasant conversation. One friend organized a visit to an art gallery on Rodeo Drive, where a young artist was exhibiting her latest works. Since my friends know I love viewing new paintings by talented artists, and enjoy painting as a hobby myself, this was a perfect idea for an entertaining evening.

As we approached the gallery on Rodeo Drive that evening, I noticed a tall man across the street intently watching our every movement. I commented to my friends that the man was very unusual looking. He was wearing a huge white turban and a long white tunic. Over the tunic was a beautiful gold brocade vest completely buttoned. I had never seen such a costume and wondered if he were a member of some religious organization. My friends suggested he was simply another unusual type seen often in big cities. I was immediately suspicious that this could be a Master, since even from a distance and in semi-darkness he looked like Maitreya.

As we approached the door of the art gallery, a young man with long blond hair, pearl-gray flowing garments and bare feet, who had been sitting under a tree by the curb, suddenly jumped to his feet and opened the gallery door for us to enter. My one friend thought he might be a beggar hoping to get a tip, yet he said not a word and bowed to us, keeping his head low. Occasionally glancing out the gallery window I noticed him sitting under the tree again. When we were about to leave the gallery he immediately jumped to his feet and opened the door for us again.

This time I was determined to see his face and learn why he was so attentive to us. My friends proceeded to walk toward our car which was parked several blocks away, but I stood firm in order to see this man. When he looked up I saw a very handsome face with a huge smile and extraordinary eyes. It was only a few years later that I saw this exact face again on the cover of a book written by an artist, Glenda Green. She claimed to have painted the exact portrait of Jesus and wrote a book called *Love Without End*, which includes their conversations as she painted.

The young blond man never spoke a word to me but pointed over my shoulder at something up the street. I turned to look and noticed a man sitting in a chair. When I looked back at the young man I thought to myself: is he pointing to Maitreya? He merely smiled, nodded his head and pointed again. I instinctively knew he wanted me to walk in that direction. As I slowly approached the seated figure I looked back at the young man several times, only to again see him smiling and nodding his head in approval.

There in front of a Bulgari jewelry store a man sat on a chair which was obviously handmade. It had remnants of tree bark and signs that a knife had whittled the legs and back supports—a sharp contrast with the jewelry store behind him. I placed the toes of my shoes within an inch of his and waited. As he slowly raised his head, I immediately recognized the face of Maitreya, although he was disguised as an old man. His slender fingers were covered with near-transparent skin and protruding veins. His hair was very white and unkempt. While the body, socks and shoes looked aged, his robe and hat were almost too perfect to be real, especially the robe, which lacked any trace of a wrinkle or pucker of the seams.

Seeing the perfection of his robe, I remembered my first impression upon seeing the photo of Maitreya in Nairobi. I had thought: if he is the Christ, and an apparition, then so are his clothes. So why is his white robe a little wrinkled and the hem a little puckered? When I later attended one of Benjamin Creme's lectures he said that some people would deny that Maitreya is the Christ simply because the hem of his robe was not perfect. That hit home!

So now Maitreya was showing me a not-so-perfect body, worn shoes and sagging socks—but the robe was absolute perfection. He seems to know our every thought and is always teaching.

Looking deeply into his eyes, my mind went quiet and I felt no need to speak or ask questions, least of all about his clothes. For a few moments I was content just to be in his presence.

Then I became intrigued by the strange assortment of religious garments he wore. His black robe was that of a Catholic priest, a cassock with a row of buttons from neckline to hem. A white Islamic crocheted cap covered his head, and Islamic prayer beads rested in his hands. On his feet were *red socks*. It was a strange combination, but all of his clothes seemed to symbolize something to me.

The black robe reminded me of my childhood days when the local Catholic priest wore a cassock in public or after service. The

Islamic symbols were probably a message to me. For while I have studied Christianity, Buddhism, Hinduism, Judaism and even the ancient religions of Egypt and Central America, Islam is one religion in which I have never taken an interest. Perhaps Maitreya was saying to me, "I am with Islam just as much as other religions."

But what did the red socks symbolize?

I got the answer when I later visited Venice, Italy. During a tour of the Church of St. Mark, the official chapel of the Doges of Venice during the days of the Republic, I was shown a huge golden screen that was built in Constantinople sometime before the 15th century. As the tour guide commented on its gemstones and portraits in enamel, she asked if we noticed anything unusual about the feet of the various figures.

There it was! Christ, the central figure, and the Emperor of Byzantium were wearing red socks. She then explained that in the early Christian church, only the Christ could be depicted wearing red socks. Later, the Emperor of Byzantium, considered by some to be Christ's political representative on earth, was also given the honor. Was the old man on Rodeo Drive telling me that by his red socks I might know that he is the Christ, and by the mix of his other clothes that he is also the one behind all religions?

Contacts with Masters increasing

Maitreya and the Masters can and do appear to people in different guises and have been doing so with greater frequency in the last few years. There is usually a symbolic message in the dress and appearance they adopt, and a contact always serves some useful purpose, very often a lesson. For example, they may test our prejudices by appearing as an individual we would ordinarily shun. But there is something so powerful in their demeanor that we momentarily drop our conditioning and take notice. In that split second we may receive an intuitive message, a blessing, a healing, a change of heart.

Another way that the Masters interact with us is to give aid in some emergency situation, as they did on my journey to Las Vegas. Numerous books and television programs recount case histories of people being saved by a mysterious stranger who seemed to come from nowhere and promptly vanished after the crisis had passed. More often than not, the grateful recipient of this service believes it is an angel that intervened, as angels have always been a part of the spiritual traditions of both East and West and are usually depicted as giving aid or uplifting humanity in some way.

Masters also appear to us in dreams, when our minds are calmer and lessons can be imparted without the interference of our continuous stream of thoughts. Over the years I have had a series of dreams where the Masters would offer some teaching. At other times they have simply made me aware of who they were.

Early in my introduction to all this I did not know their names or recognize their faces. Then, a Master appeared to me for three nights in succession, and I finally found the courage to ask his name. His reply was immediate, "I am the one you would know as St. John the Beloved."[1]

How will you recognize Maitreya?

The clearest answer to this question comes from Maitreya himself in these few short excerpts from his messages, given telepathically through Benjamin Creme:

"Many will see me soon and at first may be surprised by my appearance, for I am not the preacher of old; but have come simply to point the way, to show the path which must be trodden, back to the Source and into harmony, beauty and justice. My task is a simple one: to show you the way. You, my friends, have the difficult task of building a new world, a new country, a new truth; but together we shall triumph."

"When you see me you will know why I have come, for I shall appeal to you in these terms: save my little ones; feed your brothers. Remember that mankind is One, children of the One Father. Make over, in trust, the goods of the earth to all who are in need. Do this now and save the world. Thus shall I speak; so shall be my appeal; and when mankind has accepted this Law I shall declare myself."

"Know me by the simplicity of my utterance. Know me by the love of my heart, by my deeds of succour, by my call to all men to share and live in peace. Know me thus, my friends, and give me your help."

My next step

I realize now that if someone had approached me only a few years ago and suggested that I move to Las Vegas to take up a project to help Maitreya, I probably would have felt too inadequate, too fearful of the change, and too comfortable with my existing life to agree to such a displacement. But the Masters obviously have other work for me and so, over a period of months, perhaps years, they skillfully and patiently maneuvered me—one small step at a time—toward fulfilling my soul's purpose. We are *all* moving forward, evolving, becoming enlightened, and being guided toward a goal we may not even know exists. It is stopping on this 'path of return' to our Source that is the only real sin.

Every day we make choices that either lead us to greater awareness of who we are and what we are doing here, or we resist the forces of evolution and are eventually spurred along by pain. When a situation finally becomes *too* painful, we move on to something new. Having once grasped this inscrutable law, I have always tried to move on *before* the pain begins. There were indeed times when I felt I had no logical choice other than the immediate option offered. In hindsight, I can see clearly how each time a new door opened for me, it was a nudge in a specific direction. I could have resisted the Masters' suggestions along the way, but sooner or later I would have arrived exactly where I am today, gratefully following their path.

At this moment, I am able to perceive only a sparse outline of my work here in Las Vegas. I do know, however, that my background in diplomatic service will be useful again. This time, I will be an 'ambassador' for Maitreya, but *to whom* must remain a secret for now.

My real work will probably not begin until after Maitreya's Day of Declaration. In the interim, I lecture on the emergence of the Spiritual Hierarchy, give numerous radio interviews about the Masters and their priorities, and have now completed this book, none of which I would ever have imagined for myself or agreed to do if I had been asked too far in advance. In the next phase, the work is likely to be even more challenging, as global transformation shifts into high gear. I can only trust that I am ready for the tasks ahead.

I encourage all of you who have had experiences similar to mine, or who know in their hearts that Maitreya and the Masters are an ever-present, beneficent reality, to speak out and make it known as widely as possible, so the suffering of so many can be brought to an end, and the new era of justice, cooperation and peace can begin.

Chapter 17

❧ What does it all mean? ❧

In concluding this book I would like to divert from the personal-journal format to summarize my philosophy about where we are, as a people, and where I think we are headed. This is the message I ask you to take to heart and ponder long after you have set the book aside.

The new human consciousness

The story of the emergence of Maitreya and the Masters of Wisdom into the daily lives of all humanity is about our need for their help and guidance at what may be the most perilous time in history. The purpose of their return is not specifically religious nor is it confined to any one sector of human endeavor. Rather, they come now to teach us how to live together as brothers and sisters.

To one degree or another, we have begun to recognize that our entire civilization is in trouble. Our problems appear to become more complex and more unsolvable as time passes. That is, we appear to be incapable of solving these problems within the context of the institutions we have created over the centuries, and peace remains elusive. Therefore, the time has come for us to face the facts. And the Masters of Wisdom are here to offer their guidance and to teach us something new, the "Art of Living".

This new approach to living is now possible because a new consciousness, or change of awareness, has been gradually taking place within humanity. It manifests in how we see ourselves in relation to others and brings a new awareness of who we are and our place in the universe. Human consciousness is always changing, evolving. Sometimes the changes are slow, and at other times evolution is more rapid. Today, however, we stand on the threshold of the greatest change in human consciousness ever experienced on this planet.

As it unfolds, we are becoming aware that we live in a time of intolerable imbalances. Having lived for so long with the cruelty and apathy of a world that tolerates persecution, injustice, poverty and starvation, environmental degradation, wars of genocide and brutal commerce, we have grown weary of expecting that our problems can ever be solved. Many today wonder if there is any cause for hope.

We are not the first generation to find ourselves caught in this uncertainty and disequilibrium. Since the beginning of the human race, there must have been periods when revolutionary changes were required to meet the needs of an expanding consciousness. Such changes would have caused major chaos and culture shock before the participants were catapulted into a new way of living. It is doubtful that such dramatic changes in the past ever affected the entire world population at one time. Today, however, with nations using mass media, we have made it possible for nearly everyone to participate in the changes that the new global consciousness is creating.

What we are actually facing is a conflict between the old paradigm under which we have lived for centuries and the new human awareness which has yet to develop working institutions. In the process, there is a desperate, but ultimately hopeless, attempt in some quarters to reform the beloved old institutions to ensure their survival in a changing world. What will be needed, however, are totally new societal structures that will fulfill the needs of our new awareness. We are fearful because we do not wish to let go of the old familiar ways while the new way of living is still unclear.

In the midst of a decaying myth

Past illusions of security guaranteed by our leaders—both political and religious—are now being questioned. This is especially true in America and the wealthy European nations. The illusion or myth that all is well and we have some privileged position among the earth's population is fast being dispelled by a cold new reality. Many have already awakened to the fact that their long-held beliefs and certainties are less certain than they had supposed. But for others, this new awareness will be more difficult. As one of the Masters of Wisdom has said, "Behind it all, behind the endless and mindless destruction, this world is emerging from a dark and dream-filled sleep, the awakening from which is difficult and traumatic in the extreme."

Historically, people have always needed to believe in the power of something outside themselves, what some philosophers call a myth, meaning a widely-held view that is not actually provable. Nietzsche and Ibsen both taught that life requires such life-supporting illusions. Myths are the glue that bind people together into a cultural unit. They are the supporting foundations of any civilization and provide the moral order, the cohesion, and creative forces.

When the myth is lost, discredited or begins to fail, and there is nothing secure for the people to embrace, uncertainty and disequilibrium set in. Moral law deteriorates, and chaos reigns. We are beginning to witness these very conditions now in all our institutions.

We also have many historical examples of this cultural disintegration and the attendant culture shock. We have seen what happened when the Europeans imposed their political will upon more traditional societies in the New World, Africa and parts of Asia at the beginning of the European age of discovery. During the colonial period that followed, non-European cultures went into shock and chaos. Many did not survive.

According to Joseph Campbell, author of *Myths to Live By*, we are now in the midst of such chaos due to our own decaying myth. Referring to the fate of traditional societies in the past, he says, "Today the same thing is happening to us. With our old mythologically-founded taboos unsettled by our own modern sciences, there is everywhere in the civilized world an increase of vice and crime, mental disorders, suicides and dope addictions, shattered homes, impudent children, violence, murder and despair. These are facts; I am not inventing them."

What Campbell and others have recognized is that humanity has sensed it is entering a new state of consciousness and that the old ways, the old traditions, the old institutions will no longer serve our needs. We are caught between the conflict of the rapidly-fading illusion and the emerging new consciousness, and culture shock is evident everywhere.

Historical perspective

People often ask me if the transition from the old to the new consciousness will be painful. They ask out of fear, wondering if such pain is really necessary. I am always disappointed by this question because it reveals how little people in the affluent countries know about the daily misery in which most of the world lives. Those of us with the good fortune of living in a few of the most privileged nations, such as America and a few Western European countries, are doing fine and therefore are the slowest to recognize the need for a major overhaul of 'the system'.

Americans have been especially privileged in the modern world of 'have' and 'have not' nations. We live well and have a security few can match. We currently have jobs for almost everyone, a military more powerful than any on earth, and an economic system that provides great benefits for many of its citizens. It is not surprising, then, that many do not see the need for change. We do not focus on the fact that in the larger world there is extreme hunger, starvation, poverty, disease, and intolerance, which bring fear and uncertainty to the daily lives of literally billions of people.

The new consciousness, that deplores tolerance for greed and apathy in a world full of pain and suffering, is fast coming upon us—whether we are aware of it or not. When the 'tidal wave' falls upon us, many will surely wonder how they could have been so blind for so long. As the fledgling Christian era brought a new consciousness to the Roman Empire two thousand years ago, few privileged citizens of Rome saw it coming.

America today is, in many ways, like the old Roman Empire, whose citizens were well fed and secure. Their armies dominated much of Europe, and riches poured into their coffers. The proud Romans turned a deaf ear to the human suffering in the world they had created. Most of the empire was composed of slaves. Others lived poorly and many starved—not a very different picture from the situation in the developing nations today.

When the winds of change began to blow, few Roman citizens felt a need for change because they thought themselves too powerful and too righteous. They did not recognize the power of the new human consciousness unfolding in the early Christian era.

As the clout of that feisty little group of Christians grew, and they began to demand changes in the institutions of Rome, the empire and its privileged citizenry resisted, just as many Westerners resist the current obvious need for change. When the pressure from the Christians became a real threat, the Romans simply made a few cosmetic adjustments to appease the new Christian ideals, much like the ways in which the World Bank and International Monetary Fund respond to similar pressures today.

The Roman attempt to modify its old imperial institutions was not enough to preserve the empire. The Christians wanted *total* change, because they saw the world through a totally new set of ideals. The rest is history.

Whether in ancient Rome or modern-day America, when confronted with a new human consciousness, the old forms will be abandoned and new ones created. I suggest that this is the coming fate of our current institutions, whether they are political, economic, social or religious. There is one major difference, however, and that is the speed of such reform. What took several hundred years to accomplish in Roman times will take only a few decades to accomplish today.

Humanity at the crossroads

Maitreya and the Masters of Wisdom come into the daily life of humanity at this dangerous time because they know the problems and can offer practical solutions. It is we, however, who must make the choice to change and then be willing to do the work. We have to agree to work with the Masters; they do not force themselves upon us.

If you are a Christian and prefer to call Maitreya Jesus Christ, that is perfectly fine with him. Maitreya, however, makes it very clear that he is not the same man as in Roman times. "I came before as a man misunderstood and rejected by many. I return today, not to conquer but to lead; to show men their true nature as sons of God; to show men that they have come from a high place, indeed, and thus have far to go."

With Maitreya's help we can accelerate change and leap painlessly into a totally new time or, as he says, "...into the New Country". The choice, as always, is ours. But Maitreya and the Masters say they already know that we will make the correct choice and cooperate with them to usher in a new time that is very bright indeed.

For those who have reservations about this new time, it is important to say that the ideals set forth by Jesus nearly two thousand years ago are still very valid today. The problem is that humanity has never actually implemented those ideals. We say that brotherhood, sharing, justice and peace are our goals and a wonderful philosophy, but we never achieve them in reality. It is for this reason that the Christ has found it necessary to return to our midst and set us upon the right path before we destroy ourselves and the planet.

It is time to prepare for a total release from the failed systems and institutions of the past. We can no longer hide behind the walls of political and economic ideologies, isolationist nationalism, religious dogmas, and other divisions. We must open our hearts and minds to the new consciousness. We must allow ourselves to regain a sense of cohesion and moral order through the building of new institutions to meet the needs of our new consciousness and its goals.

I know we can accomplish this because help has arrived. I have met the Catalyst for this change, and I know, without a shadow of a doubt, that a glorious future awaits us all.

Appendix

❧ The Ageless Wisdom Teachings ❧

From very ancient times, a body of spiritual teaching known as the Ageless Wisdom has been passed from generation to generation, usually by word of mouth, from teacher to pupil. A systematic and comprehensive account of the evolution of consciousness in man and nature, it describes how the universe came to exist, how it operates, and man's place within it.

Often called esotericism, it describes the spiritual energies that underlie the everyday, phenomenal world, and is also the process of becoming aware of and gradually mastering these energies. It is the wellspring for the arts and sciences of countless civilizations, as well as the common foundation of all the world's religions.

Divine Messengers

According to the Ageless Wisdom, humanity has advanced primarily through the influence of a succession of enlightened Teachers. At the beginning of every new cosmic cycle or age—a period of approximately 2,250 years—the Spiritual Hierarchy of Masters sends one of their own into the world. The Teacher provides a new message to guide the human race into the next era. Past Teachers of this stature include historical figures such as Hercules, Hermes, Rama, Confucius, Zoroaster, Krishna, Buddha, the Christ and Mohammed.

Also known as 'Avatars', a Sanskrit word meaning 'coming down from far away', these Divine Messengers respond to the needs of humanity at the time. They are perfected examples of the divinity which lies as yet *in potential* in every human being, and their teachings have had such enormous impacts on the entire world that their names and stories are recorded and remembered for thousands of years.

The scriptures of every major religion promise further revelations with the return of a great spiritual Teacher. Today, while Christians hope for the return of Christ, Jews await the Messiah, Hindus expect Krishna, and Buddhists anticipate the Fifth (Maitreya) Buddha. Students of the Ageless Wisdom Teachings know all these as different names for the same individual—the World Teacher—Maitreya.

As stated in the Hindu sacred book, the *Bhagavad Gita*: "For the salvation of the righteous and the destruction of such as do evil, for the firm establishing of the Law, I come to birth age after age."

As we enter into such a new age, we can prepare ourselves for the Teacher's emergence in a manner never before possible. With satellite technology accessible in virtually every country of the world, we can all expect to see Maitreya and some of the Masters on international television.

We are told by Benjamin Creme that Maitreya will first appear on a major American network, then on national television in Britain and Japan. This will be followed by interviews in other countries. Then, on a worldwide broadcast, he will introduce himself to all humanity. Called the 'Day of Declaration', this amazing event will be similar to the biblical Pentecost. Maitreya, Mr. Creme explains, will speak to all humanity telepathically, as well as heal many thousands, to prove his divine nature.

It may be difficult for us now to comprehend that the outer form and its name are not important to God's plan for the evolution of the human race. What we will be learning is that we have nothing to fear and heaven to gain if we simply recognize the God within—immanent in each human being and indeed within everything in creation. Learning to transcend the form and to realize the Divine Spirit, or Self, will become a new challenge for humanity.

Earthly messengers

As humanity matures, further aspects of this previously-hidden knowledge are released in a wider, more open manner. Throughout the last 100 years, the Ageless Wisdom Teachings have been communicated mainly through the writings of four extraordinary people.

I would encourage anyone to read the works of these spiritual pioneers, since they provide a background for the new era which has already begun. Too often such inspired messengers are badly misunderstood or even vilified by those who oppose their views. Entrenched in their own dogmas, the various world religions have difficulty relating these teachings to their own. But, under Maitreya's tutelage, *all* the teachings of the ages will become clearer as we begin to recognize their similarities rather than their differences.

Helena Petrovna Blavatsky

Humanity was first introduced to the Spiritual Hierarchy in the books and teachings of Helena Petrovna Blavatsky (1831-91). In 1877 Blavatsky published her first major work, *Isis Unveiled*, which revealed her acquaintance with Eastern Adepts or Masters, and the study of their science.

Her second major work, *The Secret Doctrine*, was published in 1888. This book provided the public with a look into a variety of little-known aspects of humanity's spiritual evolution. Blavatsky claimed to be the messenger of this group of Masters, and they provided her with the material for her books. The Masters, she said, were living men she had encountered in her more than 20 years of travels around the world. She, more than anyone else, introduced humanity to the terms Hierarchy of Masters,

Brotherhood of Masters, Great White Brotherhood, and publicly presented the names of the Masters Koot Hoomi, Djwhal Khul, Morya and others.

Madame Blavatsky also performed an array of psychic phenomena that she thought would help prove the reality of unseen energetic forces not yet understood by humanity. However, these phenomena probably caused many people to question her sincerity, as the feats she performed were often too fantastic for most people to accept. She was, nevertheless, an unforgettable figure in her day, and her books are still widely available. Her great service to humanity was introducing the public to the Ageless Wisdom, the Hierarchy of Masters and the World Teacher, Maitreya. A meeting of East and West took place in her books and she showed that, in reality, the two spiritual traditions offer the same eternal message.

Helena Blavatsky was the principal founder of the Theosophical Society. After her death, others continued her work but focussed more on preparation for the coming World Teacher. Blavatsky herself had always taught that the Teacher could be expected at the close of the 20th century. Since the organization's new leaders did not believe that the Christ, Maitreya himself, would actually appear in a physical body, they searched for a suitable 'vehicle' or holy man into whom, they believed, the *spirit* of the Christ would descend. As had happened in an earlier time with Jesus, this uniting of the spiritual and physical would, they thought, produce the new World Teacher.

Jiddu Krishnamurti

In 1909 J. Krishnamurti, a young Indian boy, was discovered by leaders of the Theosophical Society and proclaimed to be the vehicle for the coming World Teacher. In 1911 an organization called the Order of the Star in the East was formed to prepare the world for this event. But, after years of meticulous preparation, Krishnamurti turned away from this role. He believed the Christ did not require him for the task of World Teacher. In 1929 Krishnamurti dissolved the Order and began his career as an independent spiritual teacher. He spent the major part of his life giving talks to millions around the globe. Recorded, these talks were reproduced in the many books and tapes which so eloquently present his views. His lectures on the understanding of life (which I consider to be the art of Self-realization), were directly inspired by Maitreya, according to both Benjamin Creme and an associate of Maitreya. Therefore, if you wish to know the basis of what Maitreya will teach in the future, you can read Krishnamurti's books now.

Alice A. Bailey

After Madame Blavatsky, a former Theosophist and the founder of the Lucis Trust and Arcane School, Alice A. Bailey, introduced a series of books, again inspired by a Master of Wisdom. In 1919 in California, Alice Bailey began her work after establishing telepathic contact with the Master of Wisdom named Djwhal Khul. He is often referred to as simply, the Tibetan. This Master dictated to her 18 books, a project which initially was expected to take about thirty years. Amazingly, the work was completed in exactly thirty years, and within thirty days after that period, Mrs. Bailey succumbed to physical death.

It was Alice Bailey who wrote the most comprehensive statement to date about the expected World Teacher, Maitreya, in her 1948 publication *The Reappearance of the Christ*. In it she explains that the reappearance of the Christ has been anticipated for decades by spiritually-minded people in both the Eastern and Western hemispheres. Although the Christ is associated today mainly with Christianity, the Christ is also the Avatar, or an aspect of God, expected under different names by the faithful in the Eastern world. For example, in the *Bhagavad Gita*, Book IV, Sutra 7, 8, are these words: "Whenever there is a withering of the law and an uprising of lawlessness on all sides, then I manifest Myself."

Helena Roerich

Helena Roerich was born in St. Petersburg, Russia in 1879, the daughter of a prominent architect. A disciple of the Master Morya, she received telepathically from him, as well as from the Master Koot Hoomi and the Lord Maitreya, a series of teachings published by the Agni Yoga Society between 1924 and 1939. As mentioned earlier, Helena Roerich passed along to President Franklin Roosevelt information from the Masters during the World War. According to Benjamin Creme, the teachings in her books were also intended "to alert the disciples to the dangers of the coming war, and to galvanize them into constructive action in line with Hierarchical intention". The first book, *Leaves of Morya's Garden I - The Call*, was dictated by Maitreya himself and revealed the plans for his imminent return. In a letter dated February 24, 1930 Helena Roerich wrote: "The epoch of Maitreya is already predicted, and the signs are already scattered like fiery seeds. Therefore, for those who follow the Cosmic Magnet, the threatening time will be full of light."

A chronology of Maitreya's emergence in our time

The following is provided courtesy of Share International Foundation:

January, 1959: British artist and esotericist Benjamin Creme was first contacted telepathically by one of the Masters of Wisdom, and three months later by Maitreya himself, who offered Creme the task of making known publicly his return. Maitreya explained: "I myself am coming, sooner than anyone thinks possible. It will be in about 20 years, and you will have a role to play in my coming if you accept it." Consenting to the unknown challenge, Creme began an arduous period of training to prepare him for the work that would ensue.

Since 1974, Creme has been the key individual speaking out on this subject, through worldwide public lectures and hundreds of interviews on radio and television, as well as through the print media. His information has been compiled into eight books and translated into numerous languages by groups responding to his message.

In July, 1977, according to Creme, Maitreya emerged from his center in the Himalayas, and traveled by plane from Pakistan to London, his 'point of focus' in the modern world—thus fulfilling the biblical prophecy that he would "come in the clouds". Returning to humanity "like a thief in the night", Maitreya established himself in London's Indian-Pakistani community, where he soon became a spokesman for the underprivileged, voicing his concern with modern problems—political, economic and social.

May, 1982: At an internationally-covered press conference in Los Angeles, Creme revealed where Maitreya was to be found. Creme challenged the world's media to mount a symbolic search for Maitreya in London's Asian community. This search, Creme said, would demonstrate humanity's willingness to invite Maitreya forward and so allow him to reveal himself without violating human free will. The media did not respond to Creme's invitation. One day after the press conference, the Falkland Islands War broke out, and no major news bureau followed through on Creme's information.

August, 1987: Creme announced: "In the coming three or four months, Maitreya will be working intensively to bring about a breakthrough in international relationships in the world." Less than a month later, political meetings between the Americans and Soviets led to the armaments agreement no one had thought possible.

April, 1988: An associate of Maitreya began regular communication with two London-based journalists, relaying Maitreya's forecasts of world events, which he makes from his knowledge of the Law of Cause and Effect. Between 1988 and 1993, this information was distributed to the world's media and published monthly in *Share International* magazine. Maitreya predicted dramatic and unexpected international events weeks, months or years before they happened. These events included: the rapprochement between the United States and Soviet Union; the growing power of 'the people's voice', demonstrating most dramatically in Eastern Europe; the collapse of communism in the Soviet Union; the release of Nelson Mandela and the ending of apartheid in South Africa; the resignation of Margaret Thatcher (a prediction made at the height of her political popularity); the defeat of George Bush in the 1992 U.S. presidential election; the peace initiatives in the Middle East and Northern Ireland; earthquakes in Armenia in 1988, and in California and China in 1989; the new worldwide focus on the environment

June, 1988: Maitreya's associate stated: "The signs of Maitreya's presence in the world will continue to increase ... He is going to flood the world with such happenings that the mind can never comprehend it." Within months, 'crosses of light' were discovered in the windows of homes near Los Angeles, and later in Canada, France, England, Japan, New Zealand and the Philippines. This phenomenon was accompanied by an increase in other inexplicable events, such as weeping statues of the Virgin Mary, apparitions of Mary and Jesus, crop circles, 'angelic' encounters and vanishing hitchhikers. As the signs continued to manifest worldwide, media coverage increased.

June 11, 1988: Maitreya materialized 'out of the blue' at a Christian prayer meeting in Nairobi, Kenya. Thousands attending instantly recognized him as the Christ. He spoke to them in their own language and many reported being cured of major illnesses. The *Kenya Times* reported that, afterwards, a man saw Maitreya take a few steps and then disappear. The *Times* photographed Maitreya, and the story was picked up and reported by international news organizations.

1991-present: As in Kenya in 1988, Maitreya continues to appear miraculously throughout the world, mainly at meetings of orthodox religious groups. Prior to his appearance in different locales, he magnetizes water in the area with healing energy. In Mexico, Germany and India the healing waters have been discovered, and millions of people have been drawn to the sites. Many claim they have been cured of illnesses such as AIDS, cancer, arthritis and glaucoma after drinking the water. Other inexplicable events continue to make the headlines, including the 1995 worldwide phenomenon of Hindu religious icons reported to be 'drinking' milk offered by worshippers and skeptics alike. Among Muslims, sacred messages formed in perfect Arabic script have been found in and on garden vegetables both in the Middle East and the UK.

Priorities: Maitreya's first priority is to inspire us to feed the thousands of people who die each day from hunger in a world with a 10% per capita surplus. Establishing proper housing, medical care and education as basic human rights are next on his list. And, at the same time, his presence will lead to a new respect for the natural world and a host of creative solutions to the environmental crisis.

Teachings: Maitreya has not come to start a new religion. He is a teacher, guide and counselor for all humanity—regardless of religious affiliation. He will show us how to apply the Principle of

Love in all our relationships—whether they are in the economic, political, educational, cultural or social spheres.

He will lead us to the recognition of our own divinity and our true identity as souls. Out of this greater spiritual understanding and creative power will come a new livingness, harmony and joy. We will learn the Principle of Sharing and a profound understanding of the oneness of all life.

The Great Invocation

From the point of Light within the Mind of God
Let light stream forth into the minds of men.
Let light descend on Earth.
From the point of Love within the Heart of God
Let love stream forth into the hearts of men.
May Christ return to Earth.
From the center where the Will of God is known
Let purpose guide the little wills of men—
The Purpose which the Masters know and serve.
From the center which we call the race of men
Let the Plan of Love and Light work out.
And may it seal the door where evil dwells.
Let Light and Love and Power
Restore the Plan on Earth.

The Great Invocation is a non-denominational, universal prayer that 'calls forth' the energies of Light, Love and Power (Will) from the Spiritual Hierarchy.

We are told that the Christ himself used the Great Invocation for the first time in June 1945, when he announced to the Masters of Wisdom that he was ready to return to the world at the earliest possible moment. This invocation was released to the world by the Master Djwhal Khul through Alice A. Bailey.

It is used daily by millions of men and women of goodwill around the world.

✺ Endnotes ✺

Chapter 4—A promise fulfilled

1. A survey published in *Time* magazine a few years ago stated that 69% of Americans believe that angels exist, and 32%, or 81 million people, report having had an angel encounter. These 'angels', I suggest, are actually Masters of Wisdom.

Chapter 6—Another meeting with Maitreya

1. I cannot speak about everything that happened at this meeting, and its purpose was not immediately revealed to me. When I first arrived in the 'other dimension' I noticed more people like myself who were probably brought there to receive the same remarkable experience. I had also seen a number of Masters during the sequence of events that followed. However, when Maitreya turned his attention to me I had the distinct impression I was alone with him and the two Masters who had been guiding me.

2. Since this was a telepathic conversation the words are an approximation of what was said.

Chapter 10—Clues from around the world

1. *Share International* magazine issues, June 1988 through November 1993.

2. *Share International*, Vol. 11, No. 1—January/February 1992, page 42.

3. "Interviews with Maitreya's Associate: Vast changes in present-day politics", by a TV journalist, *Share International*, Vol. 10, No.1—January/February 1991, page 5.

4. Stigmata is unexplained bleeding from hands, feet, forehead or chest that mirrors the wounds of the crucified body of Jesus.

5. "The Second Coming, UFOs, and the future of humanity", interview with Giorgio Bongiovanni, *Share International*, Vol. 17, No. 5—June 1998, page 8.

Chapter 12—*A new way to house-hunt*

1. According to the esoteric literature, this is the location of the 'ajna center', one of the seven main 'chakras' or energy centers in the human body.

2. George Adamski, in his short book called *Telepathy: the Cosmic or Universal Language, Part III*, explains that we humans receive messages in telepathic form. He says this is only possible when we have a mind cleared from fear, worry, anger, anxiety, and are viewing all things calmly. He suggests this often happens when we do our daily chores, because at that time we are more likely to have a composed, receptive mind. "If you watch your mind carefully," he says, "you will find many of the real universal thoughts come while you are contentedly, physically occupied." In my case it was vacuuming my carpet!

Chapter 13—*Those who look for signs*

1. "Maitreya manifests crosses of light" by Carrol Joy, *Share International*, Vol. 7, No. 6—July/August 1988, page 5.

2. "19 hours in Knoxville, Tennessee", by Buddy Piper, *Share International*, Vol. 15, No. 46—July/August 1996, page 9.

3. "Maitreya's social concerns", *Share International*, Vol. 7, No. 6— July/August 1988, page 22.

4. "...a sign that a great Soul has descended", *Share International*, Vol. 14, No. 9—November 1995, page 5.

5. "Weeping Virgin of Las Vegas", by Carole Ashley, *Share International*, Vol. 18, No. 6—July/August 1999, page 12.

6. The Blessed Mother appeared to Diego in 1531 as a dark-skinned Virgin to bring hope to the poor. She told him to go to

Bishop Zumárraga and tell him to build a church right there on Tepayac Hill. When Diego told him of the vision, the bishop insisted on a sign before he would believe. To corroborate Diego's story, Our Lady not only produced roses out-of-season but also imprinted her image on Diego's cape for the bishop to see. The Virgin's appearance in 1531 was decreed a true miracle, and she is revered as Our Lady of Guadalupe to this day.

7. "Name of 'Allah' on eggs and beans", *Share International*, Vol. 16, No. 9—November 1997, page 19.

8. "White Buffalo Calf Woman promised to return", *Share International*, Vol. 15, No. 7—September 1996, page 14.

9. "Red heifer a sign from God?", *Share International*, Vol. 16, No. 6—July/August 1997, page 16.

10. "Rainbow-coloured light emanates from Maitreya's image", *Share International*, Vol. 12, No. 3—April 1993, page 11.

11. "Miracle in Tibet", *Share International*, Vol. 18, No. 10—December 1999, page 21.

12. *Share International*, Vol. 19, No. 4—May 2000, page 19.

Chapter 14—The Master at Medjugorje

1. *Visions of the Children* (revised edition 1998) and *Meetings with Mary: Visions of the Blessed Mother* by Janice T. Connell are just two of her many books.

2. Most Catholics refer to her as the Blessed Virgin Mary. Whatever name we apply, the apparition has provided many messages for humanity, just as other miracles were occurring worldwide.

3. Maitreya's teachings have been given since 1977 through Benjamin Creme in a series of 140 messages and through interviews with Creme's Master. This information is published in Creme's books and in the pages of *Share International*

magazine. In 1988, an associate of Maitreya in London's Asian community also began to communicate portions of Maitreya's teachings to two London journalists who have made it available to the world through *Share International* magazine and a series of press releases. In addition, the teachings given by J. Krishnamurti are said to be an accurate representation of what Maitreya will teach in the new era.

4. All quotes from the visionaries at Medjugorje are taken from Janice T. Connell's book, *Visions of the Children*, 2nd ed., St. Martin's Press: New York, NY, 1998.

5. All quotes from J. Krishnamurti are from the book *The Flight of the Eagle*, Harper & Row, 1972. This book is a collection of talks given in London, Amsterdam, Paris and Saanen, Switzerland.

Chapter 16—Promises to keep

1. I eventually found that the biblical disciple of Jesus, St. John the Beloved, is now called the Master Koot Hoomi [*Share International*, Vol. 15, No. 2—March 1996, page 22]. Other Masters who work closely with humanity include Morya, Serapis, Hilarion, and Rakoczi. All of the Masters have lived among us before as outstanding historical figures like Pythagoras, Francis Bacon, Saint Paul and the Count of Saint Germain, to name just a few.

❧ Resources and suggested reading ❧

To learn about my upcoming lectures and interviews, as well as new developments since this book was published, visit my web site at:

www.WaynePeterson.com

Following are a few of the best books available to further your understanding of the subjects I have covered herein. Most of these authors have written numerous books and, in some cases, there are audio and video presentations of their talks. Therefore, I have given further contact information so you may obtain a full list of available materials.

The Reappearance of the Christ and the Masters of Wisdom

by Benjamin Creme (Los Angeles: Tara Center, 1980)
Benjamin Creme's first book gives background and other pertinent information concerning the return of Maitreya, the Christ. A vast range of subjects is covered, including: the effect of the reappearance on the world's institutions, the anti-christ and forces of evil, the soul and reincarnation, telepathy, nuclear energy, ancient civilizations, the problems of the developing world and the new economic order.

Maitreya's Mission

by Benjamin Creme (Los Angeles: Share International Fdn., Vol. I 3rd Edition 1993, Vol. II 1993, Vol. III 1997)
Each volume presents further developments in the emergence of Maitreya and the Masters of Wisdom. Subjects include: the work and teachings of the Christ, evolution and initiation, meditation and service, political and economic change, psychology, health, the

environment, science and technology, worldwide miracles. These books might be considered a chronicle of the new millennium we are entering.

Messages from Maitreya the Christ
(Los Angeles: Tara Center, 1992)

During the early years of preparation for his emergence, Maitreya gave 140 messages through Benjamin Creme during public lectures. The method used was mental overshadowing and the telepathic rapport thus set up. The messages inspire readers to spread the news of his reappearance and to work urgently for the rescue of millions suffering from poverty and starvation in a world of plenty. I have shared excerpts from these messages with you as quotes at the beginning of chapters in my book.

The Ageless Wisdom Teaching
by Benjamin Creme
(Los Angeles: Share International Fdn., 1996)

This introduction to humanity's spiritual legacy covers the major principles: the Divine Plan, source of the teaching, evolution of human consciousness, the Spiritual Hierarchy, energies, the Seven Rays, karma, reincarnation, initiation, and more.

Tara Center/Share International,
P.O. Box 6001, N. Hollywood CA 91603 USA
www.ShareIntl.org

The Reappearance of the Christ
by Alice A. Bailey
(New York: Lucis Publishing Company, 1948)

This book provided the initial information on the planned re-emergence into the everyday world of the Christ and the Masters. It describes their expected work with humanity to transform the world and bring a new peace on earth. The work was communicated telepathically to Alice Bailey by the Master Djwhal Khul, known as the Tibetan.

Externalization of the Hierarchy

by Alice A. Bailey

(New York: Lucis Publishing Company, 1957)

As the title suggests, this book provides a detailed account of the gradual emergence of the Spiritual Hierarchy, an event which has been planned for hundreds of years. It also describes the relationship among all the kingdoms in nature and all the states of consciousness.

> Lucis Publishing Co.,
>> 120 Wall St., 24th Fl., New York NY 10005 USA
>
> www.LucisTrust.org (to order books by Alice Bailey)
>
> www.netnews.org/bk/toc.html
>> (to read Bailey books free online)

Isis Unveiled

by H. P. Blavatsky

(London: Theosophical Publishing House, 1877)

This book claims to be a master key to the mysteries of ancient and modern science and theology. It was Blavatsky's first major literary work, acclaimed by the *New York Herald* as "One of the most remarkable productions of the century". Here she provides the reader with an intimate portrait of the Eastern Adepts and their science. Topics include: comparative Buddhism and Christianity, Masonry, Egyptian wisdom, Kabbala, Gnosticism, Platonic philosophy, cycles in nature, the ancient mysteries and much more.

The Secret Doctrine

by H. P. Blavatsky

(London: Theosophical Publishing House, 1888)

Blavatsky said the Masters are living men whom she encountered throughout her life and who provided her with the information for her books. Blavatsky wrote that, towards the close of each century, there is a major attempt by the Masters to help the spiritual progress of humanity. *The Secret Doctrine* has never been out of print since its publication in 1888. The book covers cosmic and human evolution, myth and archaic symbolism, science and metaphysics. An abridged edition is also available.

> Theosophical University Press, P.O. Box C,
> Pasadena CA 91109 USA
> www.Blavatsky.net
> (to read Blavatsky books free online)
> www.Blavatsky.com
> (to order books by Blavatsky
> and other Theosophists)

Hierarchy and *Heart*

by Helena Roerich (New York: Agni Yoga Society, 1924-37)
These two books are part of the Agni Yoga Series. The Agni Yoga Society publishes a number of other books including *Letters of Helena Roerich, Volumes I and II.*

> The Agni Yoga Society, 319 W. 107th St.,
> New York NY 10025-2799 USA
> Price list of available books
> from <director@roerich.org>

The Flight of the Eagle

by J. Krishnamurti (New York: Harper & Row, 1972)
This book is a collection of talks given by Krishnamurti in London, Amsterdam, Paris and Saanen, Switzerland. Although not called such, it is the teaching of Self-realization.

Krishnamurti Foundation of America,
P.O. Box 1560, Ojai CA 93024 USA
www.kfa.org

The Visions of the Children

by Janice T. Connell
(New York: St. Martin's Press, Revised Edition 1998)
This book provides the background on the apparitions of the Blessed Mother at Medjugorje, a village in Bosnia. Jan Connell interviewed the visionaries who are able to see the apparitions and has shared their experiences in this book. The apparitions of the Blessed Mother that began in 1981 have captured the imagination of people worldwide. Millions have visited the village, which has become a new spiritual mecca of our times.

The Inner Side of History

by Charles DeMotte
(Mariposa, CA: Source Publications, 1997)
To provide new insights into the history of Western civilization, Professor DeMotte combines his knowledge of history with a long-time study of the Ageless Wisdom. His book foresees future historical events in the light of the lofty goals which the Teachers of the Ageless Wisdom envision for our evolution.

Transmission Meditation groups

To learn more about this important world service activity, visit the web sites:

www.TransmissionMeditation.org and www.ShareIntl.org.

At either location you may request a referral to a group near you. If you do not use the Internet, you may mail a request to one of the Share International addresses given below:

Share International Magazine

Subscriptions and back copies may be ordered from the appropriate address noted below. A selection of past articles organized by topic may be found on the web site:

www.ShareIntl.org

(For North America, Australia, New Zealand
and The Philippines)
Share International, P.O. Box 971,
N. Hollywood, CA 91603 USA
(For the United Kingdom)
Share International, P.O. Box 3677,
London NW5 1RU, England
(For the rest of the world)
Share International, P.O. Box 41877,
1009 DB Amsterdam, Holland

Information about world hunger

The Internet site www.thehungersite.com is an innovative new tool to help feed the hungry. Visitors to the site are invited to donate a serving of food by clicking on the button. The donations are paid for by corporate sponsors. All money is given over to the United Nations World Food Programme, which endorses the site. You will also find here a great deal of useful information about the problems of hunger, poverty and related issues, as well non-profit groups who are working actively to relieve the suffering.

Tlacote tablets

Homeopathic tablets prepared from Tlacote water are available from Ainsworth Homeopathic Pharmacy, 38 New Cavendish St., London W1M 7LH, England. Phone: +44-207-935-5330.

http://www.Ainsworths.com

ᨒ About the Author ᨒ

Wayne Peterson's life of service started when he joined the Peace Corps after graduating in 1964 from the University of Wisconsin in Madison with a B.A. in International Relations. He served two years in Brazil, where he worked to create the first public welfare organization which functions to this day across that country.

In 1967 he was appointed to the U.S. Information Agency's Foreign Service by the president and served for 13 years in various diplomatic positions at American embassies in Latin America, Southeast Asia and Africa.

In 1980 he resigned from the foreign service and returned full time to Washington. He was first appointed a policy officer at USIA and then a director of the Fulbright Scholarship Program, a position he held for the next 17 years.

Wayne Peterson retired in January 1997 after 32 years with the U.S. Government. He continues his life of service, however, in another arena.

᪥

"When you see and hear me
you will realize that you have known for long
the Truths which I utter.
Within your hearts rests the Truth of God.
These simple Truths, my friends,
underlie all existence.
Sharing and Justice,
Brotherhood and Freedom
are not new concepts.
From the dawn of time
mankind has linked his aspiration
to these beckoning stars.
Now, my friends,
shall we anchor them in the world."

—Maitreya, the World Teacher

᪥